ENDO

It is truly exciting to see this wonderful book come out that will only glorify the name of our God and our Messiah Yeshua (Jesus). I have known Kokeb for many years and have been deeply impressed by his heart for the Lord. He walks in the anointing of God and desires to see revival not just upon the Jewish people but upon all nations. His testimony truly shows that God is powerful in saving and delivering people. Kokeb represents the supernatural working of God upon the Ethiopian Jews and how they are coming to salvation in fulfillment of biblical prophecy. Kokeb has gone through harrowing and dangerous life situations that most of us will never have to face. This book will inspire and encourage you in your walk with the Lord! May God bless you as you read it.

David Chernoff, Rabbi, Congregation Beth Yeshua, Philadelphia
Executive Committee and Vice President of Messianic Jewish Alliance of America (MJAA)

I have known Kokeb Gedamu for over twelve years. Kokeb is a visionary, a pioneer, a strong leader and a man of prayer. You will be deeply inspired as you read about the fascinating life of this man of faith.

Jeffrey Forman, Rabbi
City of David Messianic Synagogue, Toronto, Canada
Chairman, International Alliance of Messianic Congregations and Synagogues (IAMCS)

Yiddishly speaking, the term 'bashert' is used to convey the thought of divine intervention. Without question, the perilous and often death-defying sojourns of Kokeb and Menalu Gedamu are faith-building and inspiring. Like the prophet Jeremiah, they were called from birth to serve. And, like our first family Abraham and Sarah, their journey from Ethiopia to Israel was fraught with danger. You will absolutely marvel at God's timely provision to them when it seemed as if all hope was gone. Certainly, God's calling of this couple has been matched by His empowerment. As you read their story, may God touch your heart with the same vision that has carried this courageous family for so many years. What a supreme honor it is to cross paths with such beautiful people!

Frank Lowinger, Rabbi,
Congregation Brith Hadoshah, Buffalo, New York
President, Messianic Jewish Alliance of America (MJAA)

Journey Beyond Imagination tells a story that is familiar to those who have been to Ethiopia to observe Christian and Jewish life among those of the *Beta Yisrael* people. As such, it helps the reader learn more about a culture that is alien to most Westerners. Trials, tribulations, and blessings mark one man's physical and spiritual journey from the heart of the earth, Ethiopia, to the Sudan and then on to Egypt and Israel, where he received his citizenship. I recommend this book to anyone who wants an authentic first-person account that is emblematic of the sorrows, tragedies, and positive life-experiences that belong to our shared existence.

Robert I. Winer, M.D., Psychoanalyst, Philadelphia, PA
Honorary Executive, Messianic Jewish Alliance of America (MJAA)

Rabbi Kokeb Gedamu's story of his flight from Ethiopia, to Egypt, to Israel and eventually to the US reminds me of a similar journey the

Biblical patriarch, Abraham, endured from Ur of the Chaldees to Canaan/modern day Israel. His story will inspire you, for it is truly a testimony to God's faithfulness in the most difficult and harrowing of life's circumstances. Having known Rabbi Gedamu and his family for many years, I can vouch for his continuing faithfulness to God. His heart and ministry for his people, the *Beta Israel*, continues to be productive to this very day.

Joel Chernoff,

General Sec., Messianic Jewish Alliance of America (MJAA)

He came from poverty and persecution in Ethiopia because he is a Jew, and Jews aren't welcome there. He fled through the desert with his family and the clothes on his back. He drank water from the Nile River to survive... Kokeb Gedamu is the genuine article, the real thing... A man who has paid the price of suffering, Kokeb learned how to depend on God for miracles. Now God has raised Him up to preach the miraculous to the body of Messiah. You should not only read his book, you should invite him to minister at your church or Messianic congregation.

Joseph Bell, Rabbi/Director, For Zion's Sake Ministries, Inc.

Congregation Ari Yehudah, Bristol,TN

Kokeb Gedamu is a man of God first. His life and the life of his family is an extraordinary saga of the way in which a person's trust in God will bring one through great times of struggle. Whether in Ethiopia, the Sudan, Israel or the USA, that same trust is tried and tested many times. It is heartening to see modern-day miracles in the life of a Jewish follower of Yeshua (Jesus) the Messiah. Everyone who reads this book will be challenged to a higher connection with

God through His Divine Spirit interacting with our human lives. ***Journey Beyond Imagination*** has captured the story of a true disciple of Yeshua.

Joseph Rosenfarb, Rabbi

Beth Messiah Synagogue of Tidewater, Norfolk, VA

From Ur of the Chaldees to the Promised Land of Canaan, from obscurity to prominence, from promise-made to promise-kept, G-d called Abraham to a journey that would eventually bless all the nations of the earth. Kokeb Gedamu was born in an obscure Ethiopian village, destined to serve as a village priest, until G-d also called him to a similar journey. A remarkable story, from Ethiopia to Sudan, to Egypt, to Israel, Canada, and currently in the USA, Kokeb found the guiding hand of G-d, the eternal Navigator and unfailing Protector of his entire family. The incredible story and inspirational testimony are an encouragement to all who read this book. It speaks to the journey that we are all on, and to the promises made to us all, and to the eventual impact and blessings our journey will also bring to the world.

Judah Hungerman, Rabbi

Beth Messiah and Beth Yeshua Congregations, FL

Journey Beyond Imagination

Journey Beyond Imagination

the victorious account of the Gedamu family of Ethiopia

Kokeb Gedamu
as told by Juanita Weiss

Packaged by Fidlar Doubleday, Inc., 1515 E. Kimberly Rd., Davenport, IA 52807. 563.386.5427, 800.248.0888, x 5427, Fax 866.935.5331, www.fidlardoubleday.com

Cover design by Patricia Rasch. Layout and design of internal pages by Juanita Weiss.

Unless otherwise noted, all Scripture references are taken from the New International Version of the Holy Bible.

ISBN 978-0-9845879-0-2

DEDICATION

For our three children who were part of this journey,

Our first daughter **Ruhama**, the start of our blessing.
Ebenezer, the middle of our journey.
Tsiona, the goal of our journey to the Promised Land.
We love you!
You are the best gifts from the Lord in our life.
May God fulfill your every desire according to
His riches and will.
We are always here for you.

—Kokeb & Menalu Gedamu

To all the *Beta Yisrael* whose stories are still unwritten.

—Juanita Weiss

TABLE OF CONTENTS

ACKNOWLEDGEMENTS

...from the Gedamus

To every person, named and unnamed, who people this book. Thank you! For those who aided us in any way—from the remote village of Mo'ta, Ethiopia to the bustling cities of America—you were God's arm to us. We are here today because you were willing vessels. We will be eternally grateful to you.

For those who were our adversaries, iron sharpens iron, you gave us the impetus to move on and to be forged and fashioned in the furnace of affliction. Even though you may have meant it for evil, God meant it for good! We pray that our lives *have* and our story *will* touch you in some positive way!

To my family, my deceased parents, my mother Wobegieg and my father Gedamu in their memory, and my siblings Abren, Libanos, Assegedech, especially Rekebenaha who was like a mother to me and supplied pictures of our family for this book.

We don't have the words to express our appreciation to our dear sister Juanita Weiss who has done an amazing job at bringing our family's history to life in this book. We are really grateful for all the long days' and nights' effort you put into this book without reservation. Juanita, you will always be remembered by our family as an instrument of God. Thank you very much for your kindness and faithfulness. We also extend our gratitude to your family: your husband David, your son Jonathan; and your mother, all of whom who have been an encouragement and source of love for you. Thank you and may God bless you abundantly from Zion.

To those who sacrificed their time and effort to read, to give counsel, and to promote this book, especially:Dr. Robert Winer-Philadelphia; Rabbi Frank Lowinger-Buffalo; Rabbi David Chernoff-Philadelphia; Rabbi Jeff Forman-Toronto; Rabbi Judah Hungerman-Florida; Rabbi Joseph Bell-Tennessee; Rabbi Dr. Joseph Rosenfarb-Chesapeake; Rabbi Branny Sigal-San Diego; Joel Chernoff; Jennifer Caplan-Israel; David & Porsha Scholl-Havertown; Solomon Ashagre, and Nancy White Vencil. Thank you very much for your kindness and love for us. May God bless you richly from Zion.

To the God of Israel, You have always been faithful . . .

ACKNOWLEDGEMENTS

...from Juanita Weiss
To my husband David and son Jonathan, for all your support and understanding and for being great listeners. I love you! To my mother, Corine Tyler, who encouraged me to write and stay on task.

To my friends Beverly Howell and Danene Washington, my Ya-Ya's, who always believed that I had talent and support me in every endeavor. To my niece Nia, thanks for applauding all that I do. To my sister Barbara Davis, the first to read a portion of my manuscript and give me advice. My sister-in-law Beth Forrester, her husband Chris and their daughter Esther, whom I accosted at Thanksgiving to read a few chapters. You encouraged me and offered great suggestions. Thank you! To Duke White, my son in the Gospel, thanks for your passion for Him and for seeing the call of God upon my life.

To my friend Amy Beccerra, who wielded a mean red pen and gave many helpful suggestions, thank you. To my reading group (Katie Davis, Rebecca Kurtz, and Gailon Totheroh), thank you for the hours you spent with me, for your expertise, your insight and wisdom.

To Dr. Zemedkun and Aster Wold for being my eyes and ears to Ethiopia, for providing me with some of its local color, and allowing my laptop, my questions, and me to invade the serenity of your beautiful home.

To Bishop Michael J. Rogers & my TBT family, especially my spiritual mothers, you always believed in me, supported me, encouraged me, and sowed seeds into my life and ministry. Thank you. I will always love you.

To Rabbi Joseph Rosenfarb and my Beth Messiah Synagogue family, especially the Intercessory Prayer and Empowerment at Lunchtime groups, for your *kesher*, prayers, and encouragement. You are so important to me.

To the Gedamu family for opening your home to me and allowing me to observe your lives. I hope I have adequately portrayed your "miracle lives" and done justice to your *unimaginable* journey of hope.

To all those who read this book, thank you, and may your life be enriched by the testimony of God's hand upon the Gedamus!

And to Adonai Yeshua, the Giver of all creativity and inspiration. You are Magnificent! I am loving getting to know You! Thank You for Your patience and Your Gift!

INTRODUCTION

The story of the Ethiopian Jewish community is one that is steeped in history and intrigue. For hundreds, if not thousands of years, the God of Israel has been watching over his ancient people to bring them back home to Zion. Their sudden return which began in the early 1980's with "Operation Moses" was dramatic. It made the newspapers of the time, and the history books of today. Many would call it a modern-day miracle. Yet few of us have heard the individual stories of the journey and the struggle of those who returned.

Here is one such story that will deeply touch your heart and show God's faithfulness to fulfill his call in the lives of Kokeb and Menalu Gedamu. It is a love story, a dramatic escape through war-torn Africa, and a spiritual journey of discovering God's amazing protection, guidance and faithfulness. In pursuit of God's call to be a "Levite," Kokeb faces the refining fire of unimaginable difficulties, obstacles, opposition, and apparent closed doors. In the end, these are the exact ingredients for multiple miracles from God's hand.

I first met Kokeb and his family in Israel in 1995. He was a charismatic leader with a big vision to impact the rest of the Ethiopian Jewish community in Israel. This indomitable spirit has characterized his life since childhood and has been the success to his survival in many different situations. It has set him apart from others, and perhaps made him ahead of his time in his pursuits in Israel. However, God makes no mistakes, and when one door closes, an even greater door opens. This has been the story of Kokeb's life and today he still carries a deep burden for his home in Israel and for his own people.

I am sure that Kokeb would agree with me that the real key to success is trust in the God of Israel, no matter what the status of our birth or the challenges that life presents. This is a real-life story of destiny that will inspire and challenge every reader.

And the story continues…

Jennifer Kaplan, Israel

FOREWORD

As a retired lawyer, one of my projects is to read Pulitzer Prize winning novels, the themes of most of which express varied cultures in America. My wife and I came to know Kokeb and Menalu Gedamu and their children through Beth Yeshua Synagogue in Philadelphia. We know them as joyous, gentle, gracious, and yet determined people. We have marveled at the beauty and intellectual accomplishments of their daughter Ruhama, and observed the athleticism of their son Ebenezer, and the promise of stunning beauty of their younger daughter Tsiona. We knew some of their story, but not its entirety until we read the remarkable story of their lives set forth in this book.

I am struck by the fact that my own accomplishments in the face of what I considered obstacles pale significantly in comparison to what you will read here. I am also struck by the fact that their story is more memorable and expresses greater courage than those in many Pulitzer Prize winning novels. Their story of accomplishments in living their lives as Ethiopian Jews and sharing with others their exotic heritage reveals a culture which has not yet been explored by any Pulitzer Prize work to date.

And, most notable of all is the fact that this story is not a novel, but a true story, and these people walk among us today!

Enjoy!

David Scholl, Philadelphia

PREFACE

"Once they were kings. A half million strong, they matched their faith with fervor and out-matched the Moslem and Christian tribesmen around them to rule the mountain highlands around Lake Tanna. They called themselves *Beta Yisrael*—the House of Israel—and used the Torah to guide their prayers and memories of the heights of Jerusalem as they lived in their thatched huts in Ethiopia. But their neighbors called them Falashas—the alien ones, the invaders. ("Falashas: The Forgotten Jews," *Baltimore Jewish Times,* 9 November 1979).

In the early 1980's, Ethiopia forbade the practice of Judaism and the teaching of Hebrew. Numerous members of the *Beta Yisrael* were imprisoned on fabricated charges of being "Zionist spies," and Jewish religious leaders, *Kesim* (sometimes spelled *Quesim*), (sing. *Kes* or *Qess*) were harassed and monitored by the government.

Ethiopian Jews have been the targets of missionaries for many decades. When the missionary activity intensified at the end of the 19th century, large numbers of the Beta Israel community converted. From approximately that time until Israel began to actively help the Jews immigrate, members of the Beta Israel community have abandoned their faith. Some did so because they were pressured or persuaded by the missionaries; others responded to social pressure, and some may have viewed conversion as a way to improve their economic condition (for example, they could then own land). These people who had once been Jews, or, more often, whose ancestors had been Jews, are referred to as the *Falash Mura*. The *Falash Mura*, however, did not refer to themselves as *Beta Israel* until after the Jews had begun to immigrate to Israel.

Most Jews who converted to Christianity joined the Coptic Orthodox church. The Ethiopian Church was part of the Coptic Orthodox Church until 1959. One of the few pre-colonial Christian churches of Sub-Saharan Africa, it has a membership of about 40 million people and is thus the largest of all Oriental Orthodox churches. The faith and practice of most

Orthodox Ethiopian Christians reflects Jewish and Christian influences. For example, their churches consist of three main parts, with the Holy of Holies as its center, just like the Jewish Tabernacle, and their priests, called *Kesim* or *Quesim*, are considered Levites, *kohanim*.

The historical data concerning how a Jewish population first came to settle in Ethiopia is scant due to the lack of written records and the regional prevalence of oral traditions. There are however many theories, of which three are the most widely accepted:

1. The Ethiopian Jews are the descendants of the lost ancient Israelite tribe of Dan.
2. They may be the descendants of Menelik I, the fabled son of King Solomon and the Queen of Sheba, as set down in the folkloric, biblical and aggadic Ethiopian Kebra Negast.
3. They might be descendants of Jews who left Israel for Egypt following the destruction of the First Temple in 586 BCE.

Regardless, for thousands of years, Jews in Ethiopia maintained a strict pre-Talmudic biblical Judaism. They kept *Kashrut* (Jewish dietary laws), the laws of ritual cleanliness, and observed the Jewish Sabbath and festivals. The *Kesim* (religious leaders) were respected as the rabbis of each community and presided over festival services in the ancient liturgical language of *Ge'ez*. They passed down Jewish tradition orally and maintained the Jewish books and torah scrolls that some communities had preserved in *Ge'ez*.[1]

Here is the story of one of them.

Ephesians 3:20-21

Now unto him that is able to do exceeding abundantly above all that we ***ask*** *or* ***think****, according to the power that worketh in us, Unto him be glory in the church by Christ Jesus throughout all ages, world without end. Amen. (KJV, boldface added)*

Now to him who is able to do immeasurably more than all we ***ask*** *or* ***imagine****, according to his power that is at work within us, to him be glory in the church and in Christ Jesus throughout all generations, for ever and ever! Amen. (NIV, boldface added)*

Now to him who by his power working in us is able to do far beyond anything we can ***ask*** *or* ***imagine****, to him be glory in the Messianic Community and in Messiah Yeshua from generation to generation forever. Amen. (CJB, boldface added)*

Places of Kokeb's Travels in Ethiopia

- **Mota**—a town in southwest Ethiopia Located in the Misraq Gojjam Zone of the Amhara Region
- **Debre Markos**—a city in east-central Ethiopia, located in the Misraq Gojjam Zone of the Amhara Region
- **Addis Ababa**—is the capital city of Ethiopia
- **Bahar Dar**, also Bahir Dar (Amharic "sea shore")—a city in northwestern Ethiopia and the capital of the Amhara Region.
- **Gondar,** also Gonder—Located in the Simien Gondar Zone of the Amhara Region, north of Lake Tana
- **Metema,** also Metemma—a town in northwestern Ethiopia, on the border with Sudan
- **Wonja Showa**—town near Nazret in the Oromia province

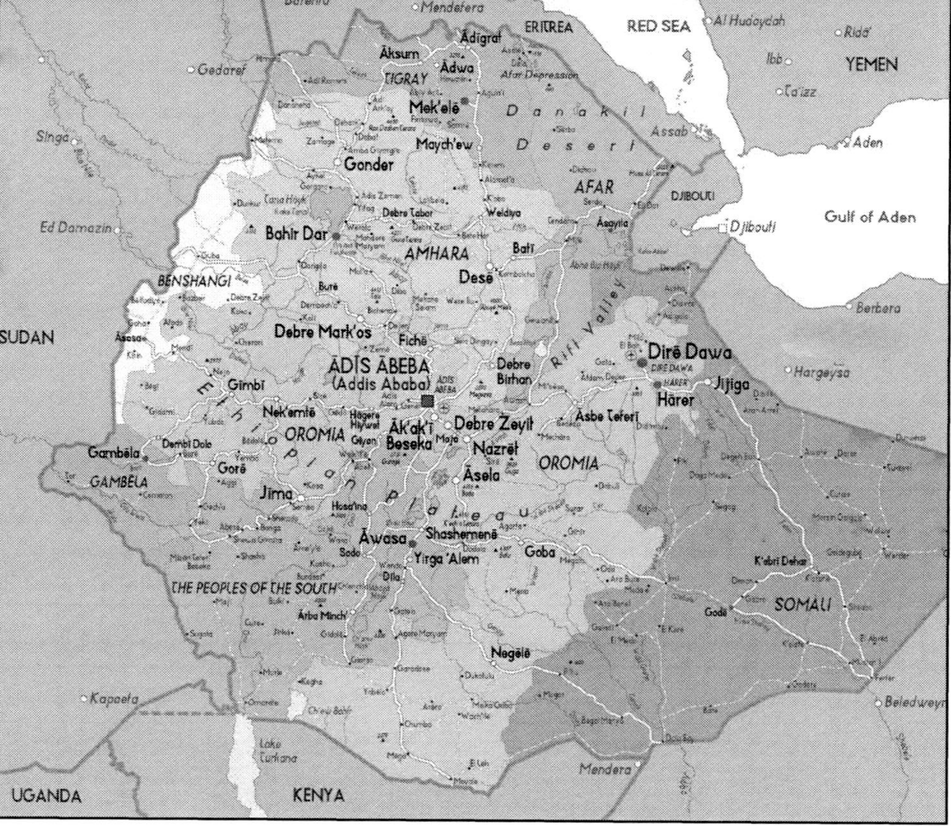

Map from Ezilon.com used by permission.

Part I

Beyond Asking...

Chapter 1

Mo'ta Village, Ethiopia—June 19-20, 1966

WHY WON'T THE BABY COME? WOBEGIEG WONDERED. Sweat beaded upon her forehead, the growing weight of each bead forcing the water to run in rivulets down her face. The midwife dabbed the laboring mother's brow.

"He's waiting for just the perfect time," the experienced midwife responded, as if she were reading Wobegieg's mind.

Unmoved by the midwife's intuition, Wobegieg still wavered between the worst and the best outcomes. She knew the truth in the village stories of women giving birth in mud huts to babies already dead ... of mothers dying with their babies inside of them ... of mothers holding babies with malformed limbs or faces. Even with the latter, the babies were given additional attention ... according to Ethiopian custom, they deserved more. Wobegieg (which means "beautiful" in

Amharic, the ancient language of the Ethiopians) lay in the bed behind the "meketa," the bamboo partition that separated the parents' room from the large open area. Her husband Gedamu had constructed the bed on which she lay. To make it, he had killed the cow, gathered its fresh leather, and cut it into long strips. He had soaked the strips in water until they were the desired softness for his wife. He had woven them checkerboard fashion and finally nailed the pattern to a wooden bed frame. After his labor, Gedamu had welcomed Wobegieg into his home; now, with her labor, she was about to bring forth another seed of her husband's family on that bed.

Rumbles of thunder shook the mud-and-hay huts of Mo'ta Village. It was "keremet," the season of the "big rains," which lasted from mid-May to September. Lightning set the inky night sky ablaze and shone like filtered gold through the cracks inside Gedamu's fragile dwelling. Their three children had stayed awake for as long as they could, expecting to greet their new sibling, and now they lay asleep in the open area of the hut on the remaining "medevs," mats of mud and stone.

This was Wobegieg's third day of pushing and coaxing so that the baby would break forth. "O, God of Israel," she prayed, "let my baby be healthy." She was going to have a child with **Qess** *(which means 'priest') Gedamu, the man she had married, and the man she loved. Wobegieg's every moan was an eruption of pride in the blessing of bringing forth a child for him.* **Let it be a man child**, *she prayed.*

Despite three days of labor, Wobegieg resolutely hoped for the best. She knew there were no doctors available in the village who might offer her baby a better chance. So she prayed. Was the answer in the torrents of rain that fell, turning the paths between the huts into small rivers? Was the answer in the thunder that struck and quickened fear in every part of her being? Or was the answer in the flashes of light, like angels dancing in the darkness?

She remembered watching her abdomen swell with the life inside of her, and with each inch swelled her gratitude to God for allowing her such a blessing. As was the custom, she had to eat anything that she craved throughout her pregnancy, even if providing it for her meant extra work for her husband or children. If she did not eat what she craved, the people of Mo'ta believed the baby would be born with a mark that would blemish the smooth bronze skin so prided by the Ethiopians. So she ate for her baby. In the last two days, she had forced herself to eat even when the thought of eating turned her stomach.

In the greater Ethiopia, beyond the small villages, prosperity had come because of the rule of Haile Selassie I, the emperor and self-proclaimed Lion of Judah—he had given his people hope. He had defied the advances of Italy and promoted independence and peace to his people and the world. Did his rule not bode well for her family also—for her and her new child? So she ate and hoped and prayed.

"Just a little more pushing," the old woman said.

"I am so tired," Wobegieg moaned.

"I believe your baby is coming soon."

"I believe he must," she said softly. She knew that if her baby did not come soon, she would not have the energy to send him into the world. "What time is it?" she asked the midwife dabbing at her rivulets of sweat.

"It will be light soon," the midwife said.

"Uuuuhhhhhhhhhhhh," Wobegieg let out a scream. Her eldest daughter, Rekebenaha, jumped from her bed and ran to the bedside of her strong mother; she would be there to witness my birth. She would be there to tell me all that occurred that night. She would be my eyes and understanding before I had sight.

The midwife quickly slid into position, coaxing, cajoling, and coaching my mother until life burst forth. My father, *Qess* Gedamu, waited in one hut with the village men, while the women waited in another. He had been there for two nights, but he would go during the day to visit Wobegieg. He had blessed her, prayed for her, and left her in the hands of God. He raised his head at the sound of the nighttime screams, screams he had heard before, so he waited, tuning his ear for the sound that caused every Ethiopian father to swell in pride.

The midwife pulled me forth. With a gentle tap on my behind, my mouth opened, my lungs cleared, and I greeted the world with my cry. She washed me, and gave me to my mother. Wiping her hands on the cloth hung from her waist, she walked over to the entrance of the hut. Once outside, she cupped her hands to her mouth and raised her voice in the long awaited *elelta*, the joyous chant/cry that announces to all that a child is born and the time of celebration has come. Her skilled tongue vibrating against the roof of her mouth had made that cry hundreds of times before.

The welcomed sound drew Gedamu quickly from the mens' hut. In a sweeping motion he looked up at the star that greeted him and then continued on to his hut, sloshing through the small rivers. The women had awakened immediately from their anxious slumber and now poured into the hut to see the newest member of Mo'ta Village.

"You have a son!" the midwife proclaimed to Gedamu, leading him to his wife. "What will be his name?"

My mother handed me to my father, the Coptic priest.

"The first thing that I saw outside the hut was a star, a morning star," Gedamu said. Its brightness drew my glance upward and followed me as I came to you, Wobegieg, and our son. I shall call him 'Kokeb [star] Tsivaha [morning].' He was my star at the beginning of this day."

"Kokeb is our fourth child and second son. May he be a light to many," Wobegieg said.

My father took me, held me in his arms, blessed me, and dedicated me back to God. He called me *Kokeb Tsivaha* and gave me his first name—Gedamu—as my last name. To my parents, I was that 'morning star' which burst forth during the "big rains" of June 1966.

The women of the village would dance and sing, rejoicing for three days in celebration of my birth. Each day they would make coffee, bring food, and rejoice with my mother—in hopes that she would forget her pain and remember the joy that she held in her arms. I, my parents' "morning star," would grow dim many times and be drenched in many *keremets* before I reached the brightness for which I had been born.

This is the story of my beginning.

Chapter 2

Mo'ta Village, Ethiopia—7 Days Later

"YOU MUST EAT *GENFO* FOR TEN DAYS," THE MIDWIFE TOLD MY mother. The porridge-like dish of wheat, barley, and oats is high in protein and often fed to new mothers. "You have to keep up your strength, for there is still much more to do. You will soon feel like new again."

"Is he a healthy boy, my little Kokeb?" my mother asked the midwife every day.

"He is the healthiest boy I've seen in a very long time. But you must eat."

"I prayed that he would be healthy."

"I know you did. All mothers do."

"I know, but not all mothers get their wish."

"Eat," she said, handing my mother more *genfo.*

Seven days later she was already feeling a little stronger. She would indeed need her strength because this was the day of the cleansing. The hut had been prepared for the entrance of the presiding priest, one of several, along with my father, on staff at the village church. The time had been set. Tawny-colored villagers formed facing rows that stretched to the doorway of the Gedamu hut. The Ethiopian priest arrived as punctually as a cock's crow, his face the color of polished brass, framed by a salt-and-pepper lamb's wool beard. Like a tribal king, he walked between the lines. Dressed in white cotton pants, a flowing gown, and full turban, the priest carried a small jar of holy water, a cross, a prayer book, and the authority of God to drive away unclean spirits and to pronounce clean that which had been defiled by the birth process. The family emerged from the hut as the priest entered.

He went through the cleansing ritual with the natural rhythms of a bird feeding and preening its young. He took the holy water and sprinkled it on the furniture in the hut, reciting a blessing each time. Calling my mother, he showered her with three heavy sprinkles of holy water. He placed the cross before her; she kissed it three times, and he pronounced her clean.

Everyone waited in silence befitting the sacred event. After what seemed like hours, the priest emerged from the hut, and joyous voices jolted the atmosphere. The time of feasting had begun. For three more days the village would celebrate with dancing and singing. My mother would abstain from all work and labor for forty days according to the Biblical mandate of Leviticus 12:1-4:

> The LORD said to Moses, "Say to the Israelites: 'A woman who becomes pregnant and gives birth to a son will be ceremonially unclean for seven days, just as she is unclean during her monthly period. On the eighth day the boy is to be circumcised. Then the woman must wait thirty-three days to be purified from her bleeding. She must not touch anything sacred or go to the sanctuary until the days of her purification are over...'"

My mother's family and the village women helped her with household chores and meal preparation. My people believe that if a woman re-entered society before forty days, she and her baby would be plagued by an evil spirit.

The next day—the eighth day—would be another day of feasting. It was the *megerez*—the day of circumcision. As the God of Israel had made this covenant with Abraham thousands of years before, so the seed of Abraham continued to keep the agreement. My sister Rekebenaha helped my mother dress me in white clothing. The priest came again to bless the process. He called forth the Levite, a skilled cutter, to cut away the foreskin. I cried when the incision was made, Rekebenaha would later tell me. Then the incision was seared with fire to stop the bleeding. Without the benefit of anesthesia or a pain reliever, I would cry for weeks, as long as the pain lasted. Amid my pain, the village celebrated the birth of a boy, the continuation of tradition, the repopulation of the village of Mo'ta, and the growth of the Levite *kohanim*, priests.

Nearly a century before, Christian missionaries attempted to convert Ethiopian Jews. The majority resisted and maintained their Jewish faith. Some did convert, however; these were called by outsiders *Falash Mura,* which became a title that we despised. Those outsiders would have considered me *Falash Mura,* for I was the son of a Jewish man who was a *Qess* in the Coptic Orthodox Church. We held fast to the Judaic practices of circumcision and ritual cleansing.

For thirty-two days after my mother gave birth to me, neither she or my father could enter the church until they were deemed entirely clean from the pollution of birth. I, my parents' morning star, would not be brought outside into the natural light for the same number of days for fear that the brightness would weaken my eyes. The next year my mother became pregnant with my sister Abren. Sadly, forty days was not enough time for my mother to regain her strength and return to village life. The *genfo* did not have the miraculous healing qualities for my mother as it had with her previous four births. Six months after Abren was born, my mother died.

So I never got a chance to look upon my mother's face or to smell her fragrance—with memory. Those things were lost to me. There were not enough maternal caresses to help me remember what they were like. But her name means 'beautiful' and every part of God's creation reminds me of her —a flower, the rain, the sky…'the morning star.' That beauty has helped me overcome some of the most difficult times of my life.

Chapter 3

Gondar City, Ethiopia—September 21, 1967

ONE THING THAT I AM QUITE FAMILIAR WITH, HAVING LIVED IN THE hills of Ethiopia, is the circle of life. One neighbor kills a lamb for a festive meal, and the same day another neighbor announces that his cow bore two calves. Dirges are sung for an old man who is carried to his final resting place, and the same day a midwife chants the *elelta*.

A baby girl was born in far away Gondar City in 1967, a year after my birth. She would become my wife, Menalu. The God of Israel, in His great wisdom, would recycle life and death, and as one female child entered this world and eventually my life, another woman, my mother, in 1968, left this world but never would she leave my life.

Menalu's birth city of Gondar was much bigger and

more modern than Mo'ta. It was a town on whose streets one would see horses, buggies, cars, and buses. It was a town which housed an airport bigger than that in Mo'ta. Menalu had access to doctors, but her parents chose to use a midwife because the women of the village were more comfortable with the traditional method of birth. Menalu would not be born in a hut like me, but in a single floor "house" made out of wood and stone, a house with divided rooms. Her mother, Astatek, would use one of those rooms as a birthing chamber for the only child that she would give her husband Melesse.

Astatek had known since she was a little girl that Melesse would be her husband; their parents had arranged the marriage. For a long time, marriage was just a distant thought to Astatek; but before she knew it, it had become a reality. Already much older than Astatek, Melesse had two daughters by his ex-wife, two and three years older than she. In the first year of marriage, Astatek was giving birth to her first child.

"What shall be the name of this child?" the midwife asked, giving the child to the Astatek.

"Look how beautiful she is!" exclaimed Astatek.

Melesse looked at his new daughter. "Look at the difference between me and my wife, he said. "I am old. She is young. Now my young wife has a daughter. What will people say? 'Menalu.'" he said. "That's what we will call her. 'What will people think? What will people say?'"

After the birth, the midwife moved deftly to the front door where she sang the elelta, that joyous chant/cry that summoned all the women to welcome a new daughter into the world. At once, the villagers emerged from their huts and came crowding in to celebrate Menalu's birth with her parents.

Melesse fixed his eyes on Astatek. He covered his head with his *kippah* (the Jewish man's prayer cap) and spoke in Hebrew the ancient blessing of our people: "God of Abraham, Isaac and Jacob, bless my daughter as you have blessed Sarah, Rachel, Rebekah, and Leah. Please make her fruitful, and bless her descendants with land and prosperity. May our daughter open the doors for us to go to Jerusalem in the Promised Land." His blessing became more than a prayer; it became a prophecy. The God of Israel would hover over that word and indeed perform it.

The Ethiopian Jews, also called the *Beta Yisrael* in Amharic, which means "House of Israel," always reflected upon the hills of Jerusalem although they had ever seen them. As they lived and worked in the mountains, one of the core values of their Jewish belief, prayer, and daily life was the desire to return to "Zion"—to look upon its hills. Melesse saw Menalu as God's answer to this age-old desire of our people.

After Menalu's birth, Melesse's job assigned him to Metema, a little town situated on the border of Ethiopia and Sudan. As a customs officer, Melesse collected taxes from merchants who traveled in and out of the country and who traded with neighboring regions. Years later, Sudan would become as important to Menalu and to me as Ethiopia and the cities of our birth.

Metema was a rural community, devoid of all the amenities found in Gondar. Astatek's family knew that life in Metema would be difficult for Menalu, so they did not allow her to go. When Melesse went away without Astatek and Menalu, they went to live with Astatek's family in Gondar. Melesse resented them for not coming to live with him in Metema, so he did not write to them or send money. Astatek's parents took care of Menalu and arranged another marriage for Astatek to a man named Azanaw. Astatek had another child with her new husband, a daughter Kenubshe, who was four years younger than Menalu. While Menalu remained with her grandmother in Gondar, Astatek lived with Kenubshe and Azanaw in a smaller town outside Gondar.

When Menalu went to visit her mother and sister for two weeks, Astatek saw a side of her new husband that compelled her to make a life-changing decision. For five cents, a person could by a loaf-and-a-half of bread. Azanaw bought five cents' worth of bread and brought it home to his family. Kenubshe, although younger and smaller, was given the larger piece of bread. Menalu, the smaller piece.

"Why would you do that?" Astatek asked him.

"Menalu is not my daughter. Let her father take care of her. I will take care of my daughter," Azanaw said.

This was too much for Astatek to bear, so she took both her girls and returned to Gondar to live with her parents. A year later, Melesse came to visit Astatek. He saw that she had remarried but he wanted her back. Without consulting her parents, Astatek divorced her husband and moved to Metema with Menalu and Melesse, who also took in Kenubshe as his own child.

Melesse's farm in Metema included a main hut for his family and several huts for the workers and their families. There was no plumbing, so they gathered water at a well with the use a donkey, while the workers carried water pots on their heads.

Menalu's father grew cotton, corn, and *simsim*, or sesame, which he sold in the city so that it could be used to make oil. Most homes used sesame oil for cooking. Livestock abounded: horses, camels, donkeys, goats and cows, so there was plenty of meat, milk, butter, and cheese. Since there was no refrigeration, they gave to village families most of these commodities.

Menalu remembers that on full moon nights, they sat outside eating roasted corn and talking as families talked, catching up on all that Menalu had done in Gondar. They , however, never wandered from the safety of the hut. Hyenas and lions lurked in the distance, waiting to satisfy their appetites.

Centuries before, my ancestors were among the *Beta Yisrael* who were forced to convert to Coptic Orthodox Christianity; Menalu's parents were different. Since they did not convert, they practiced strict Jewish customs. For thousands of years, most Jews in Ethiopia maintained strict Biblical Judaism, by keeping *Kashrut* (Jewish dietary laws), the laws of ritual cleanliness, and observing the Jewish Sabbath and festivals.

Because Melesse kept a kosher home, obeying the Old Testament *Kashrut* laws about the preparation of food, he would not eat the food of non-Jews nor would he eat with them. Every meal received the typical Jewish blessing: *Baruch atah Adonai, Eloheynu Melech Ha olah hamotzie le chem min a haretz.* "Blessed are you, O, Lord our God, King of the universe, who gives us bread from the earth."

Everyone in the town knew that Menalu's family was Jewish even though there were not many Jews in Metema—most of them lived in Menalu's father's birth city of Quara. Jews generally kept their Jewish identity a secret—some attended church, married Christians, and assimilated into the culture. Menalu's family did not. It would be this identity that Menalu would keep secret, until one day, when revealed, it would unlock many possibilities for her future.

Chapter 4

Mo'ta Village—Kokeb, Age 5

WHEN MY MOTHER DIED, *ABBA*, MY FATHER, TRIED TO KEEP OUR family together, but with all of his obligations, he could not. He could not remarry and remain a priest, so having a new mother was not in our future. *Abba* did the only customary thing that any priest could do—he divided my siblings among their godparents. My baby sister Abren, my eldest sister Rekebenaha, my older brother Libanos, and my older sister Assegedech were sent to different relatives.

He took away Rekebenaha, the only mother I had known. Many nights I longed for her when I slept on my *medev* alone, or cried tears that a mother's hands should dry, or experienced fears that only a mother's caress could soothe.

I remained with *abba*. He believed God called me to the life of the priesthood, so who better to raise me than a *Qess* himself. But he was one who worked all day, studied when he could, and carried out his Levitical duties on *Shabbat*.

I was left in a village of mud and hay. That's what most of the huts in Mo'ta were made of, and Papa was an expert at making those huts. As a Coptic Orthodox priest, he gained a great deal of respect and a small salary, but to support his family, he built huts.

"Can't I come with you?" I begged almost every morning as my father gathered his tools. When he left, I knew I would be asleep when he returned and not see him until morning.

"No, Kokebtsivaha, you must complete your studies."

I can remember kicking at the dust many times in disappointment as I started my ten-minute walk to school, ultimately meeting up with the other boys.

My father integrated me into church life long before anything else could be a first memory. When the rooster crowed at 3:00 a.m., the church doorkeeper rang the big bell three times every fifteen minutes to call the priests to prayer. The church held a special service called *Sahatat*—prayer and special songs—in *Ge'ez* from 3:00 a.m. to 6:00 a.m. My father wanted me to understand the prayer life of a priest, so sometimes he took me with him.

"Kokeb," he said nudging my arm. "It's time to wake up. We must go to prayer."

I struggled out of bed, wrapped myself in church garments, held my father's hand and allowed the cool early morning air to wake me momentarily. The ten-minute walk to the church was done in silence, my father preparing himself for prayer, and me wanting to go back to sleep. After praying as long as a young child was able, I would then curl up on one of the back seats and fall asleep.

When I did not want to go with my father, I stayed at home, though it was not a safe place for a five year old because the huts did not have very strong doors. Anything could wander in. In the pitch black, I snuggled up into my *medev,* a mat of mud and stone, and tried to sleep amid the nocturnal sounds of animals hunting and crickets and cicadas chirping. Sometimes my father would wake me before he left, sometimes not.

Once, in the dark before dawn, the smell of wildness pervaded my hut, and something moved stealthily in the dark. My father was gone and had not awakened me. I knew *something* was in our hut. Something that should not have been there. I dared not move. It was a wolf searching for food. All I wanted to do was cry out for my father as my heart thumped like a pounding fist in my chest. I could run but where? I would never see what was in front of me. *My God, it is walking near me. He's coming over to the* ***medev****. He knows that I am here. Lie perfectly still. Let him sniff you, but don't move. He wants to rouse you to action so that he can pounce on you.* But like a termite, tunneling deep within its mound, I had burrowed down into my *medev*. The intruder could not see me, I wished frantically. I was resolved not to move a muscle. I just had to lie completely still and the invader would leave once it discovered that there was no food in our hut.

But he was still there, inching frightfully closer. "Go away!" I screamed at the top of my lungs. My hands clutched my ears. My eyes were squeezed shut, and my feet pedaled wildly! "Go away! Go away! Go away!" When I finally calmed down and looked around, the intruder was gone.

My father had said that I had a destiny, so I knew it was the God of Israel who protected me those many times I was left home alone.

I was the priest's son, so when most of the other children wore modern clothes, I stood out by wearing *qess'* garments, priestly clothing, made for me by my father. When most children played, did chores, or studied in a modern school, I, and about twenty other boys my age, walked to the home of our *MerGeta*, teacher. *MerGeta*s were like Levites, but they could not become Coptic priests since they were divorced. Instead, they served as teachers to young boys being trained for the priesthood. Like my father, however, they were well learned in the study of Scriptures. I remember once my *MerGeta* telling his students, about twenty of us at the time, to stay away from the *debtera*. While these Levites were very educated and learned in orthodox language and customs as well, they used their knowledge for evil through witchcraft and fortunetelling.

While the modern school children learned their studies in Amharic, I embraced my studies in *Ge'ez*, the ancient

Ethiopian language used only by priests for liturgy, prayer, and study. None of the children outside of the priesthood knew this language. I was taught to read the book of Psalms and the Gospel of John in the ancient language of Ethiopian priests. My studies were always punctuated by a wish to be with my father, but as much as I wanted to be with him, the lure of the church's inner sanctum always filled me with an awe and wonderment I could not explain at that age.

The church was a big, beautiful circular building made of wood and hay. Its interior walls were decorated with ornate paintings of angels and saints. The cavity of the building was partitioned into three circular sections. The outer circle was divided into two parts at the middle. This represented the outer court where the men sat on the right and the women on the left. Inside was another circular section, also divided in the middle. The wives of the priests and Levites sat here, on the right; the priests, Levites, and deacons on the left. In the middle was another circular section. At the center stood a table on which rested a box containing the Ark of the Covenant, and inside that was the Big Book. This was the Holy of Holies, and my studies took me on a journey toward this place, which I gazed upon with deep reverence.

Each step of my journey drew with it the expectation that the Almighty Himself would emerge from the shadows. In the Bible, only the high priest was allowed to enter the Holy of Holies, and similarly, only a few were allowed to enter this sacred place in church: my father and his deacons. Although we were taught to revere the Holy of Holies, the combined feelings of fear and intrigue were overwhelming.

I longed to be the one who could enter, to gaze upon holiness, to be embraced by the presence of God. At the age of six, it was never a toss-up as whether to be with my father or with all this sacredness. I always preferred to be with my father . . . until I walked into the building. *Abba* had always told me we were the children of *Wolte Yisrael* (Mother Israel). He said that we were from the tribe of Levi so we were born to be *Qesim*, priests. I knew nothing of *Wolte Yisrael* and the only other fact I knew about being a Levite was that one could never remarry. Beyond that, I knew nothing else, but whenever I walked past the Holy of Holies, I had every intention of finding out everything *abba* had not told me.

Chapter 5

Debre Markos—Kokeb, Age 10

WHEN BIRDS HATCH, THEY WAIT DAYS TO BE ABLE TO LEAVE THE nest, spread their wings, fly, and find their own food. I was like a bird as I studied the ancient religious texts in *Ge'ez* from the age of five until ten. At the age of ten, I could be ordained as a deacon. This ordination ritual was part of my leaving the nest. The Holy of Holies would no longer be off limits to me. It would no longer be a mystery. Leaving the nest to get there—*that* was the most difficult part.

"You are about to do something that will affect your lives forever," my *MerGeta* told fifteen of us boys the day before our journey. "You are going to Debre Markos to be ordained as deacons. It will take three days to arrive there and we will go on foot." The idea excited us; anything the *MerGeta* said that we would do we *could* do. "We will walk through the forest," he continued, "but only during the day. We will sleep in neighboring villages at night. Remember, you are doing this for the Lord. He will repay you for what you do for Him."

We all arrived at the *MerGeta*'s house very early the next morning. Wow! Three days of walking through the forest! We carried *besso*, roasted barley powder that we would mix with water to become a paste, and *kolo*, roasted barley, chick peas, and safflower. This would be the staple of breakfast, lunch, and dinner during our trip. Those commodities would feed our bodies, so we also carried items that would feed our souls. Every boy being ordained as a deacon brought several prayer books, as all three days of our adventure, morning, noon, and night, would find us reciting our prayers.

Ethiopia is considered the land of eternal spring. The difference in elevation determines the temperature, so our trip would take us through various climate ranges.

As we passed through villages, the weather, for the most part, was comfortable, but a few times I had to wipe beads of sweat from my forehead. Young farmers, some younger than us aspiring deacons, tended their fathers' sheep and goats on sprawling pastures. Cows, sheep, and oxen grazed on meadows and hills awash in the steady Ethiopian sunlight. We saw many women carrying water jars or wood on their heads and backs as easily as extra limbs, their colorful garments wavering like rainbows against the green landscape. We passed men, some leading a cow, goat, or sheep to the market in the next village to sell, buy, or trade. They were donned in white cotton *gabis,* long swaths of cloth thrown over each shoulder, material that helped them adjust to the day's varied temperatures.

Then we entered the forest which was like walking into the blast of an air-conditioned store (something I would not experience until much later in life). It was a welcomed relief from the sun, but after a while, I found myself drawing my clothing close about me. The forest teemed with life. Everywhere we saw rabbits scurrying across its leafy floor searching for a tasty morsel of grass. Birds colored the forest and piped their cheery music. The nests of weaverbirds dangled like upside-down hearts from skinny tree branches. Foxes were as afraid of us as we of them, and the *MerGeta* would say, "That's only a fox." As we continued through the forest, we saw castles of termite mounds stretching their turrets to the sky, and birds perching on them as wary sentries.

Acacia trees grew in abundance. Although their leaves were delicately small, the trees' branches were numerous, forming a canopy over the forest and protecting us from the sun's harsh rays. From their bark protruded hard, sharp thorns waiting to pierce naked skin. As the birds brought color and music to the forest, the Eucalyptus trees, with long, glossy green leaves, brought a spicy fragrance, and their thorny branches the reality of pain. We tried to keep our hands to ourselves, as my *MerGeta* had warned us.

When my *MerGeta* knew that night was approaching, he stopped at the nearest village and asked for lodging. It was the custom of the hospitable people of Ethiopia that strangers would find comfort on their journey. They washed our feet and invited us to share some *injera,* a spongy, fermented flat bread made out of nutritious *teff,* tiny, round grains high in protein, minerals, and fiber.

Our kindly hosts also invited us to participate in a *bunna* (coffee) ceremony, a true sign of Ethiopian neighborliness. They lit one fire to burn incense and another to roast the coffee beans and grind them into a powder. The ground coffee was added to a *jebena* pot and set over burning coals. The coupling of the fragrance of incense and coffee filled the hut with a hearty aroma. The first round of coffee was usually very strong and served to the adults. The second and third servings were weaker, so we children also enjoyed the hospitality. We slept on the floor of the huts under borrowed goat or sheep skins. Some huts had *kotes,* small bunk beds built onto the sides, for just such occasions as hosting visitors.

Becoming a deacon was not without its dangers. Part of the journey through the forest had to be made at night. My *MerGeta* knew that bandits lay in wait during the day, hiding in the man-high grasses. The villagers warned us that those thieves would rob us of all that we owned, even our lives. Could our journey be at the same time that bandits would choose to strike? Every sound startled us, and the moon's light cast shadows on trees and bushes, giving each a ghostly appearance.

My *MerGeta* forbade us to touch any of the foliage. He

said that some of the leaves were poisonous, and if we but smelled them, they would bring us death. So we were careful to keep our hands by our sides and our breathing almost imperceptible around certain plants. I held my breath intermittently. I walked with my hands frozen to my side in fear of touching a poisonous plant. When we came out of the forest and the sun smiled upon us, I, too, could smile.

Traveling through the Choke Mountains was an arduous undertaking, especially for me. My legs were covered with blisters and mosquito bites. My mouth was parched and I was hot all over—not just because of the heat. I must have touched something or smelled something forbidden, even though I thought I had walked with great caution, because I was terribly ill on that third day when we came out of the forest. The fact that I was young, frail, and hungry did not help matters either.

When we arrived at the next village, my *MerGeta* decided that I could not continue the journey in my condition, so he left me with a family who could take care of me until I became well. The woman of the house soaked a cloth in cool water and placed it on my forehead to bring down my fever. To rid me of the vapor that had invaded my nostrils and sickened me, she forced me to take the traditional remedy. She made a compress of dried plants which she ground into powder, and wrapped in a cloth, forcing me to keep it under my nose. With threats of imminent death if I did not faithfully continue the regimen, she urged me to drink a hot tea made from roots collected from medicinal trees that grew in the forest. I followed her instructions every day for a week until she saw a marked improvement in my health. Then, as my *MerGeta* had instructed, the villagers sent me to Debre Markos with another group passing through on their way to the ordination ritual.

When I arrived in Debre Markos, the capital of Gojam Province, I was amazed at the city. It had running water, cars, and electricity. The newness of all that I saw sapped my fatigue and gave me new energy.

I went to the Coptic Orthodox Temple where I was met by the Bishop's Assistant. Every day, boys from different villages came into the Temple for ordination. About 150 of us sat in the main sanctuary waiting for the assistant to call the names of our villages. When he finally called "Mo'ta," I, along with several of the other boys, went to the front and lined up. He asked my name.

"Kokeb," I said.

"Say '*Malka Yesus*' for Monday," he commanded. For every day of the week, there was a special "Prayer for Yesus" we had memorized as part of our training.

I recited it confidently.

"Recite the Psalms portion for Monday."

Every portion had to begin with "Hallelujah,' so I started, "Hallelujah! Blessed is the man who—"

Bringing my memorization to an abrupt stop, he motioned me to sit in a chair to his right.

To all of us seated on his right he said, "Tomorrow you will see the Bishop. Make sure that you wash your bodies, change your clothes, and consecrate yourselves. If you do not wash your whole body, make sure to wash your hands, feet, and face. You are expected to fast, so do not eat anything before you come tomorrow morning to the church."

As we filed into the church the next morning, we were told to sit down front. Although much larger, the church was arranged like the one in Mo'ta: three circular sections. We faced the most important section of all, The Holy of Holies. After a while, we were motioned to stand. The Bishop emerged from that place like a dark angel, his black bishop's hat peaked on top greeted the heavens. A long white beard framed a bronzed face with perfectly chiseled features. His long black robe indicated that he was too important for this world. This man was here to guide us safely from this world to the next. With holy fear we beheld the sight for which we had walked miles and miles, and for which I had almost died.

He prayed the prayers that were so familiar, but coming from him, the blessing stuck deep within me. It was one experience that I would never let go of. Then the assistant told us to sit. One by one we came up, kissed the Bishop's feet and knelt before him. As we knelt, he placed both hands on my shoulders and blessed me. He lifted me up, extended his ring to me, and I kissed it with great holy fear and awe. He served us holy communion together. Then, he led us to the most exalted place in the building.

We had been told about this moment. It was the reason our stomachs were rumbling in hunger from fasting—because if we came before the Holy of Holies unclean and defiled, we would be struck down like our ancestors in the wilderness. We were told that although we could not see the angels they were there, and they would strike us dead if we entered this room frivolously. We had to say "*Malka Yesus*" to prepare ourselves for entrance. We were led in. The place was dimly lit by a handmade candle. The curtain was drawn and we saw it—the Ark of the Covenant that held the Big Book; it rested on the *menber,* the table that must have been nearly *as* holy, for it held the holiness of God, hidden to all others, but no longer to me. Although I could cast my eyes upon the Ark, I would never be able to touch it, as only the priest could.

I was given a certificate with my name on it—Kokeb Tsivaha Gedamu. Then I returned to Mo'ta and served the Lord for two years as a deacon in the Orthodox church. But Mo'ta, my nest, could never hold the hatchling forever. The reverence for the sacred found in my ordination ritual would be the driving force for a flight that would take me far from the familiarity of the nest where I was born.

Chapter 6

Addis Ababa—Kokeb, Age 12

EYELIDS COVER YOUR EYES, BUT YOU CANNOT SEE BEHIND THEM. Although they protect your eyes, they prevent sight as well. That's how it was with Mo'ta. I lived there. It was like my eyelid—a part of me, but it was blinding me. It protected me, but it did not allow me to see beyond it. When I was twelve, my friend Fikere approached me with a proposition that would raise my eyelids forever.

"Let's ask our fathers if we can go to the modern school," Fikere suggested.

"My father would never let me," I said.

"We have to ask anyway. Do you know what they do at that school? They wear modern clothes. They play outside. They laugh a lot. They learn their studies in Amharic, a language everyone speaks, not in *Ge'ez.* And they get to learn a foreign language, too—English."

I am sure he knew I was moved by what he said. All of it excited me!

"What do you say? Let's ask."

I agreed.

After dinner, I gathered the nerve to ask my *abba* the question to which I already knew the answer, but I would try anyway. "*Abba,* there is a new school opening in Mo'ta. It's a modern school. Fikere and I would like to go. May I?"

"Kokeb, you have been dedicated to God. Remember Samuel? You are not like other children. You are a Levite."

"But, *Abba,* no one speaks *Ge'ez* outside of the Church."

"Because *Ge'ez* is not for the common man. It is used only for man's communication with God."

"But—"

"No, *but's,* Kokeb Tsivaha. You are a Levite. That is all I am going to say."

With my father's refusal, the next step was obvious. We had to run away. If we could not attend a modern school, we would go where we had more freedom. When we met later, we decided to leave the following day. Instead of going to my studies as usual, I would meet Fikere and that would be our last day in Mo'ta. In our studies and from village merchants, we had heard about Addis Ababa, the capital of Ethiopia. Life would be easy there and we could learn modern things. Yes, that was where we would go!

We started out walking, following the highway, and

after half a day we waved to a truck. The driver did not want to give us a ride but we pleaded with him, telling him, "We came from the capital to Mo'ta to study *Ge'ez* to be priests, but now we want to return to our families. We just want to go home. Please take us! Please," we begged, "please."

The driver's heart was softened by our plight, our pleas, and our age. He agreed and told us to get on top of the truck. Although we had never been in a truck before, we knew something was wrong with riding on top of it. Since we were not tied down or buckled up, we were in constant fear for our lives during the entire ride

We rode for three days over dirt roads and rough terrain on top of the truck. We traveled over flat highlands that went on for miles, then suddenly dropped into steep lowlands. The truck sent muddy water from streams and shallow ravines flying in our faces and showering us in sticky slime. When the driver grew tired, he would spend the night in a hotel, leaving us a bite to eat and allowing us to camp out on top of his truck. The stars painted a captivating picture in the nighttime sky, but we believed that the stars above Addis Ababa were far more intriguing than the ones we saw above us now. Each morning that the driver started the truck, we knew we were in for another adventure.

Given our lies and running away, it was a miracle that we did not fall from the truck and break our necks. Every jiggle, every sway, every stomach-unsettling toss and near-death experience was reduced by the anticipation of getting to

Addis Ababa. We focused only upon the positive things: getting jobs, earning money, and seeing a world of which we had only dreamed. We passed small hillsides that gave way to hulking mountains, which stood like giant baboons guarding the landscape behind them from whatever was approaching from the front.

"When we get through Dejen," the driver shouted at us from inside the truck, "you really had better hold on. We will be going down the Blue Nile Gorge and I cannot stop." We were frightened, but how could the rest of the trip be more frightening than what we had already survived?

A long narrow street led us into Dejen, the banana city, the beginning of the Blue Nile Gorge. Locals, carrying their wares and guiding goats, donkeys, and cows, walked to and fro as we maneuvered between them, their garments creating a single colorful tapestry against the landscape. Adults stared and children waved at Fikere and me on top of the lorry. Bananas grew in abundance everywhere. We could smell the sweetness in the air as we drove through the city. On the other side, aloes and succulents dotted the flatlands.

"Hold on!" the driver yelled. We were at the Gorge! We clung with a viselike grip to the truck's sides. Our bodies thumped against the roof of the lorry. It was as if we were flying on bumpy turbulence, but without the ability to soar above it. The *thump-thump, bumpety-bumpety bump* of the wheels against the descending rocky walls of the gorge shook things inside me I had never known existed. Because my eyes were glued shut, the sight of the cavernous gorge is not even a memory to me today, only the swaying and thumping of my body and the jarring flips of my stomach. "God, forgive us for lying!" Fikere and I shouted. We knew that we would never live to see our families again. And Addis Ababa—was it only a dream? Every bump or dip sent the truck into an aerial free-fall and our bodies mimicked the truck's up-and-down jostling. Finally, I sensed that we were no longer going down. WE WERE GOING UP! The truck's transmission roared as it tried to make the ascent. Did we dare look behind us? If we had, we would have seen a sheer descent that ended in the Blue Nile River below. The sight alone would have been enough to send us to early graves! The shut-eye-squeezed-tightly approach was the only answer to living through this nightmare.

Finally the truck was on level ground, and we opened our eyes. Needles of pain seared our eyes from their opening and from the light, but what we gazed upon made up for the whole ordeal. Addis Ababa, capital and largest city of Ethiopia! I had heard that it was right in the center of the country, and there is was, Addis Ababa perched some 8,000 feet above sea level. To get here, we had crossed many streams and traveled winding roads around its many amazing hills. *Addis Ababa*—the words means "new flower" and that's how we saw the world open up to us, like a flower opening. Tall concrete buildings, not mud and hay huts, seemed plastered like a painting against the sky. Paved roads unfurled before us, not muddy streets. Cars zoomed past us, more cars than we had ever seen in all of our twelve years.

The driver stopped at the Mercato, the vast open-air market located on the western side of the city. Flourishing industries sold leather, metal, and textile goods alongside regional agricultural produce: coffee, tobacco, and dairy products. The air was filled with the sweet and over-ripe smells of fruit—all kinds, colors, shapes, and sizes. Vegetables galore! Fish filled the stalls: long ones, short ones, smooth ones, scaly ones, snub-nosed ones, some thick and some as flat as *injera*. Clothing! Honey! Everything one needed was sold here at the Mercato! In various languages and dialects, vendors shouted the worth of their wares at passersby and customers.

We thanked the driver and ran off to find my uncle. The first place we went was Gojam Veranda—people from all over Gojam converged upon this shopping center. They came and went, they renewed old acquaintances and established new friendships; they shopped, strolled, dined.

My father had always spoken of his brother-in-law Admite and the jewelry shop he owned in the capital city. With him, we might find food and a place to sleep—and maybe even a place to work. Every day we set out to find him in so large a city, but to no avail, so for three days and nights we lived like *berenda adary adari,* the homeless. We begged for food from restaurants, and when people brought their leftovers or threw away scraps of food, we were counted among the beggars and those who fought for resting spaces around the Veranda proper. Having only the clothes on our backs, we huddled up together during the cold nights and prayed that no one would bother us. Every day we set out to find my uncle and on the third day, there was success.

After the difficulty of the last three days, seeing my uncle was very disappointing. He did not recognize me, nor did he believe that I had traveled so far with a companion so young. Several times he asked me to leave his shop against all my pleas and protests. I knew I had to convince him of my identity and quickly, as we had nothing to eat and nowhere to go. He *had* to believe me. After I recited to him my whole family tree, he was convinced that I was his nephew. He could not believe that I had traveled so far with only a companion my age. He took us in, fed and clothed us. He also let me work in his store as an errand boy. Sometimes I cleaned his store or did other odd jobs around the shop.

Every day, Fikere would come to visit me while I worked in my uncle's store. He had found a job as a houseboy in the home of a wealthy family. The second month I spent in Addis Ababa, my uncle sent me to work in a friend's auto repair shop. After that, I never again saw Fikere. I heard after many years when I was eighteen that Fikere had joined the Ethiopian military.

People from nearby villages, and even as far away as Mo'ta, would come to the Mercato. It was through those from Mo'ta that my father discovered that I was in Addis Ababa with his brother. By the end of three months, my father had come to fetch me. I was afraid to see him, but I knew that I did not want to return to Mo'ta and to my old way of life. Too much had been opened up before me! He promised me that he would not punish me if I returned with him.

Then he said something that mattered to me more than punishment or freedom from it. He said I could go to the modern school that I wanted to attend. It was all I could do not to drag my father out the door.

Chapter 7

Mo'ta—Kokeb, Age 12½

I RETURNED TO MO'TA, ECSTATIC THAT I WOULD SOON BE ATTENDING the school of my choice.

"Kokeb, come let's talk."

"Yes, *Abba,*" I said sitting next to him.

"I checked with the school and the year is almost over. Why don't you wait until next year to start?" I grimaced. "Then," my father hurried on, "you can start at the beginning. You can finish your studies here at the church and be ready for the next school year."

I did not doubt that my father would follow through with his promise. I trusted his word. I just did not want to wait, so I reluctantly agreed to enter school the following year. My expectations were shattered again…

And again…Dergue soldiers began attacking villages

in Ethiopia in 1974. Dergue was a communist military junta that came to power following the overthrow of Haile Selassie I. Dergue, which means "committee" or "council" in *Ge'ez*, is the short name of the Coordinating Committee of the Armed Forces, Police, and Territorial Army, a committee of military officers. They were fighting the rebels in the smaller towns that supported Haile Selassie. The Sudanese came to help the rebels, the Ethiopian Democratic Union (EDU), but the combined forces were no match for Dergue and the Russian Secret Police. From 1974 to 1987, Dergue executed and imprisoned tens of thousands of its opponents without trial and expropriated the land, as communism ruled Ethiopia.

My father knew that the small village of Mo'ta was a stronghold of rebel supporters of Haile Selassie, so when he heard that the army was approaching, he advised me to go to Gondar for safety. Among the masses, I had a better chance for survival. He found merchants who were going to sell spices in Adet, a city about forty miles away. He also gave me money and food for the trip. For a day and a half I walked over mountains and hills. My journey to Debre Markos when I was ten had prepared me for the perils I would encounter as I traveled on foot—all except one, the Abay River. To get to Adet, we had to cross this rushing river.

Oh, there was another way to reach Adet, but that was to travel another day to go around the river at its widest part. As children, we had bathed in, played in, and watered our livestock in the river near Mo'ta, but one thing I never did in it was swim…because I had never learned to swim. The merchants made sure their wares were tied tightly to the mules and donkeys so that they could easily cross the river at its narrowest. Then the merchants tied a rope around my waist and pulled me across the river like the parcels of merchandise they were carrying…only their parcels did not scream and panic and believe that they would die!

When we arrived in Adet, I used some of the money my father had given me to pay my fare for a bus to take me to the small town of Bahar Dar, where I stayed for several days. Someone on the bus said, "That's Lake Tanna." I had heard about our country's largest lake. Tiny islands jutted out like the humps of hippos. Merchants in papyrus boats carried firewood or fish to the regional market in the city. Like others passing through, I would take my baths in Lake Tanna's beautiful blue waters and watch as the pink pelican searched for their food.

The city was peaceful. Palm trees bordered the streets and locals scooted by on bicycles no doubt loving the flat land. As I was going into a diner to eat lunch, the usual cool breeze glided over Lake Tanna and caressed me in its freshness. Some of the locals who were eating in the diner said that a helicopter had landed in the town. I had seen helicopters flying high above us, but had never seen one close up. So of course I was curious. One of the locals said something else that aroused my curiosity. He said, "There are *ferenge-och* there too." I had heard the word, but had never seen one. *Ferenge-och* are the white people who were revered by Ethiopians. In our folklore, touching one would be like touching an angel. We had heard that they lived in the larger cities in Ethiopia, but the communist government had ordered that any *ferenge-och* from America or Europe could no longer enter Ethiopia. Only communist *ferenge-och* had the freedom to come and go as they pleased.

According to the local, however, they were "over there." He pointed out the window near where I was sitting. A helicopter was with them. He said something else that sealed my destiny and further proved to me that the God of Israel had preserved my life and was orchestrating my steps: "One of them is from Canada and the other from Switzerland."

My father had told me that Rekebenaha, my oldest sister who was living in Gondar, worked for a Canadian, a *ferenge*. Before he could say more, I was out of my seat and running in the direction the man had pointed. There they were, and there was the helicopter. I was out of breath. I was about to see angels and the cloud that they had flown in on. I discovered later these men had come to Ethiopia to perform agricultural studies with soil testing. Beside them was an Ethiopian translator. "Could you ask something for me?" I asked the translator in Amharic.

"No, they do not want to be bothered," he replied.

"Please, I am trying to find my sister," I begged.

The translator was not very pleased that I wanted their

attention and wanted to send me away. But I was persistent, for I had come too far to be pushed aside. The *ferenge* looked at me and spoke to the translator. I had never seen skin so white or eyes so translucent; no wonder we had come to believe that they were angels.

"My sister works for a Canadian in Gondar," I blurted out quickly. "Her name is Rekebenaha. Do you know her?" The translator shared the information but clearly without the same level of importance as I had communicated it to him.

The foreigners shook my hand and said their names. I forgot all things of the past in that moment. Not only did I get to meet *ferenge-och*, but I got to touch one, too! Immediately, my vision of the future was enlarged.

The translator looked more surprised than I when they said, "Yes." Rekebenaha worked for their boss! Every time I look back on this meeting, my faith in the All-Knowing God of Israel increases.

The miracle did not stop there; the *ferenge-och* gave me the directions to the place where my sister worked and ten Ethiopian *birr* to purchase a bus ticket to get there! Another miracle from the God who had ordained that my life be a light to many. To this day, forty years later, I remember this divine appointment and the generosity of Dr. Amerdlan from Canada and Mr. Hanss from Switzerland. May the God of Israel bless them!

The next day I took a bus to Gondar in a four-hour drive. It was an amazing city. Horse-drawn buggies, the main source of transportation, *click-clucked* down busy streets. Huge stone buildings reached into the sky. I had to take a look around the city before I set off to find my sister. I just had to see The Royal Enclosure that I had read about in school. It was the former residence of the great Ethiopian kings. Five stone castles were surrounded by high stone walls. Raised walkways and tunnels connected them; as I walked through I was transported back into my country's past. The oldest of these is the Castle of Fasilades, rough hewn stone piled layer upon layer. As I touched it, I thought about the men who were involved in every stage of building The Enclosure. I climbed to the upper story and there was Lake Tanna, serenely reposing in the distance. Finally, I asked someone where I could find the address that the *ferenge* had given me.

I arrived at the gate of a huge house. I told the gatekeeper who I was and whom I had come to see. A woman, tall and lovely, walked out. Although I saw my resemblance in her, she did not see hers in me, for she walked past me and back into the house. She had mistaken me for a beggar because of my soiled and tattered appearance. When I spoke with the gatekeeper again, he went to get her. I told her who I was. "*Ethalen*," I said. It means "my sister" in Amharic. It was customary that we did not call our older sisters by their names. "I am Kokeb, your brother." We had not seen each other in nearly eight years. She said my name repeatedly—it was like music, like the ancestral cadence of drums and dance. Our tears mingled. Our laughter was a chorus! She was my sister, but in the short time we had shared in Mo'ta, she had been the only maternal figure I had ever known. I had lost her; now she was mine again.

We could not wait to catch up on the lost years. We talked for hours! Fortunately her boss was away and would be away all week. She took me upstairs in this house of many rooms and told me to get into the shower. This was so different from the river where I used to bathe as a child, or the outside shower that I had used in Debre Markos, or the blue waters of Lake Tanna. Rain from inside the house pelted my body. Soap created bubbles on my skin. Had I died and gone to heaven? Had I just battled the obstacles of life to get to a place that I had never imagined? Hadn't I met an angel who pointed me in this direction? Hadn't I met my dear sister Rekebenaha here? Yes, this must be heaven!

Knowing I would not be suitably dressed to meet anyone, she took me into town and bought clothes for me, telling me her story along the way:

She had been living with our uncle, but he made her work a lot and didn't take care of her very well. She went to a Catholic charity school, Debre Selam which adopted her and taught her English. A Canadian man saw how intelligent she was and requested the privilege of teaching her. He then took her in and raised her as his daughter.

"Can't I come to live with you, sister?" I asked.

"He will not allow it," she said sadly.

"But why not?"

"I told him that I had no family in Gondar. If I now tell him about you, he will think that I lied to him. I am frightened at what he will do if he thinks I am lying."

"Will he hurt you?"

"No, I do not believe that he will, but he may force me to leave and then where will I go? Besides, you are not allowed to enter the *ferenge*'s house."

"I will not ask you to do anything that will harm you."

"We will ask Uncle Zeru. He has no children. Maybe you can live with him. I will take you there. The Lord brought you here and He did that for a reason," she said.

Uncle Zeru took me in and cared for me. My uncle lived near Tsadiku Yochanes, a modern school where I enrolled. After being tested, I was put in the third grade. I was finally doing what I had wanted to do for so long—I was attending a modern school! Now to see if it met my fascination! So there was no time to waste. I had to learn. Halfway through, I was promoted to the fourth grade.

Although I had the opportunity to attend a modern school, it came at a high price. My uncle's wife sold *tela,* a homemade fermented drink, out of her house, which was one room divided into many. In addition, my uncle would go into the neighboring villages to buy *teff,* wheat, sorghum, or lentils. Then he would return to Gondar to sell the grain. What did all of this have to do with me and the huge price I paid for my education? I went to school in the morning, and came home in the afternoon, not to study but to work for my uncle. I carried fifty kilograms on my back to the granary. I stacked the bags and carted them to the marketplace. Being able to excel in school and keep up with my studies—that was another miracle.

It took Egypt, the wilderness, and Kadesh Barnea to prepare the Children of Israel for the reality of the Promised Land. Mo'ta, Adet, Bahar Dar—it took the experiences of these unforgettable places to bring forth a dream that would be realized in Gondar.

In my waking hours, God was at work to bring forth a greater reality, not just to my dream, but for the future he had prepared for me. Tsadeku Yochanes School, a modern school that had been the object of my longing, was the key to that future.

Part II

Beyond Thinking...

Chapter 8

Metema—Menalu

FOR WEEKS, RADIOS BLARED THE NEWS THAT THE DERGUE SOLDIERS were advancing. Villagers had prepared bunkers in the dirt and inside mountain walls. They loaded each one with canned and dried goods just in case they had to hide while the Ethiopian Democratic Union (EDU) fought off the soldiers. After all the seemingly futile broadcasts, the village of Metema began to carry on life as usual.

But ask anyone who has lived through a life-and-death ordeal what the beginning of that day was like. Go ahead. Ask. He or she would tell you that it was a normal day. The sun came up, people rose from their beds, they went to work, and did chores; babies cried and mothers fed them. That's how it was for Menalu the day the Dergue soldiers came into

Metema. She got up, went to school, returned home to help her mother Astatek, and went to bed. There were no telltale signs that this would be the day unlike all days; it would change her life forever.

Ack-ack-ack—ack-ack-ack, the machine-gun fire sounded, waking up Menalu and the villagers of Metema in the middle of the night.

"What's that, Mama?" Menalu asked.

"The soldiers are coming! They are attacking the edge of town. Sleep now but be prepared to run in the morning," Astatek told her two daughters. Fortunately, they lived in the middle of town. *Even so, how could I sleep,* Menalu remembered, *when frightening nighttime noises had replaced the familiar, safe sounds of crickets and frogs.* At that moment, Menalu longed for her father, but he had gone to Gondar, to get his retirement papers in order. She felt, somehow, that if he were with her, he would keep her safe. What will he think once he hears the news about his home, his village, and his family? she thought.

Astatek, like the other villagers, prayed all night that the village would somehow escape the worst. Menalu covered her ears, trying to keep out the sounds that would make a nightmare out of her world. She was not even sure if she and her family would live through the night.

In the morning, the announcement that the villagers feared came: "Get out! We are defeated. Metema has been defeated. The soldiers are coming!" Astatek gathered her family. They held hands, her mother, Kenubshe, and Menalu.

"When I give the signal, run," she told them. "Do not stop, do not look around, just run. And if anything happens to me, do not stop running."

"Mama!" Menalu cried.

"Do you hear me? Do not stop! Both of you promise me that you will not stop." Menalu and Kenubshe looked at each other, sobbing. "Promise me," Astatek said, with frightening seriousness.

"I promise," they chorused.

Standing at the door of the hut, peering out, Astatek saw villagers scurrying like army ants, all toward an unknown destination. "Now," she said, and off they ran. Shots were fired around them, over their heads, bullets whizzing past like deadly hornets.

They were lucky to find a shelter because once the shelters were occupied, the squatters did not make room for new tenants. Kenubshe crawled in, then Menalu, and then Astatek. Stuffed like a yolk inside of an egg, they cowered and clung to each other. People who did not reach a shelter ran to the stone mountains seeking refuge or in the very familiar recesses of the valleys. Anything to shield them from the bullets or put distance between themselves and the approaching army.

Menalu could tell when a spray of bullets missed its target and when its deadly appetite had been satisfied. Metema would never be the same again because so many of those who had peopled the village were now dead.

The fighting lasted a week, and at the end of the week, Menalu, her family, and others fled the city. With only the clothes on their backs, they walked aimlessly, as far from the city as they could. When they heard gunfire, they fell to the ground—like dead weight—as if they had been shot. Menalu lay on top of her mother to protect her. What would she have done without her? Where would she have gone? How could she take care of Kenubshe? Menalu was ready to take the very first bullet.

During a moment of silence, Menalu and her family began to run again. Then the ominous sound of jets jolted them with fear, and some of those fleeing fell dead from the sudden shock of the noise of bombs pounding the landscape. The village of Metema was in flames behind them.

After a day of traveling, they reached an International Red Cross helicopter. The workers gave them food, clothes, and powdered milk. The helicopter took the most needy first —those who were sick, old, or pregnant. The others, like Menalu and her family, waited their turn. So many of them had swollen feet from running and walking on rocks and sticks and uneven ground. With no clue to what the future held and no where to retreat, Menalu and her family spent the day with the others sitting or milling around the lake, and the night asleep under trees, huddled together, defiant against separation, even in sleep. It did not take long for the workers and the refugees to realize that powdered milk was a foreign substance that hunger had forced them to introduce into their feeble bodies. Many wretched with horrible vomiting and relentless diarrhea.

After eight days, the Red Cross helicopter brought Menalu and her family to Gondar. When the people of Gondar had heard of the siege of Metema, those with relatives there had traveled to the airport every day, hoping for good news. Menalu's father was one of them.

Menalu and her family moved in with Astatek's family. Because there was no opening in the school, Menalu had to wait five months before she could attend Tsadeku Yochanes school, the same school I was currently attending.

To bring together Ruth and Boaz, God used famine, deaths, a woman's love for her homeland, and a daughter's love for her mother-in-law. For Menalu and me, He used Dergue soldiers and the spread of Communism.

Chapter 9

Gondar—Tsadeku Yochanes Elementary & Middle Schools, Fasilades High School

"KOKEB, YOU'RE LATE AGAIN."

I could easily have told my teacher the truth—that I was late because I was helping my uncle and aunt with chores—but after the first time, that excuse was never good enough for him. There was just no time to study at home.

"And where is your homework?"

I could tell the truth again, but what would have been the point? He had heard it before. I held out my hand to take the "whipping" I knew was coming my way. The long, thin tree would be a deterrent for what—not performing my required duty, helping my uncle and aunt?

Despite my tardiness and lack of homework, I grew in favor with God and man. By the fifth grade, I was much bigger than the other children. And although I was constantly tardy and not always successful in completing my homework, my teacher knew that I was more attentive than most of my classmates. I guess they knew that because I never wanted to sit in the back of the classroom, and I did not want to be disturbed by those around me. I always sat toward the front.

The discipline I learned through my religious studies as a young boy and the drive that caused me to travel over 500 miles on foot at this point in my life led to a promotion as the Fifth Grade Class Monitor. Every morning that we arrived, we filed into class and sat at benches, each accommodating three students. The table part of the bench was a desk, so the lid could be lifted, and the compartment, called a *morable*, was used for storage. About eighty-two students of different ages and skill levels were assigned to a classroom. So my duties as a class monitor were very necessary. I assisted the teacher in controlling the class, and I also had the duty to punish any unruly child. I was the disciplinarian. Whenever someone got out of line or was playing or inattentive, I whipped him or her. I meted out lashes as easily and swiftly as they had been meted out to me.

Even today, a pastor who is now in America remembers that I whipped him when he was younger. We shared a hearty laugh over the belief that God used one of those whippings to bring him into the fold.

At the beginning of class, two children raised the Ethiopian Flag, and we were required to sing the National

Anthem. Because the Dergue Communist government was in power (1975-1992), this is the anthem we sang:

> Ethiopia, Ethiopia – Ethiopia, be first
> In socialism – flourish, be fertile!
>
> Your brave sons have made a covenant,
> That your rivers and mountains, your virgin land
> Should be a sacrifice for the unity of Ethiopia, for your freedom,
> To your honour and renown!
>
> Strive forwards on the road of wisdom,
> Gird yourself for the task,
> For the prosperity of the land!
>
> You are the mother of heroes – be proud of your sons,
> May your enemies perish – may you live for ever.[2]

When King Haile Selaisse I (1930-1975) was in power, mellow Ethiopian voices blended to proudly sing these words:

> Ethiopia, be happy
> thanks to the power of God and your ruler.
> Your brave citizens are unanimous;
> your freedom will never be touched,
> as your mountains are defiant
> and your natives do not fear any enemy.
> Long live our victorious ruler
> to the glory of our country.[2]

It would not be until 1992, after the overthrow of the Communist government, that the eighty ethnic groups in Ethiopia could sing this anthem:

Respect for citizenship is strong in our Ethiopia;
National pride is seen, shining from one side to another.
For peace, for justice, for the freedom of peoples,
In equality and in love we stand united.
Firm of foundation, we do not dismiss humanness;
We are peoples who live through work.
Wonderful is the stage of tradition, mistress of proud heritage,
Mother of natural virtue, mother of a valorous people.
We shall protect you - we have a duty;
Our Ethiopia, live! And let us be proud of you! [2]

At the end of forty-five minutes, the bell would signal the end of each class. Sometimes we would stay in our classrooms and the teachers would come to us. When the students changed classes for special training in reading or recess, we formed a single file line.

During recess, the girls usually played volleyball, the boys' soccer. Our soccer ball was made up of rags and old clothing rolled tightly together and tied with string. Sometimes it was just a sock stuffed with rags. We formed teams of four or five boys. On a dusty field, we would kick, run, sweat, and have to stop several times to mend the ball. We all knew about the professional team in the city that played with a real leather ball on a real field, though most of us would never see them play. For forty-five minutes during recess, we became those professional players. We loved it so much that we planned to meet after school to continue the carefree excitement of a game of soccer. I could rarely attend, but for the few occasions that I did, I was momentarily transported into the world of a child that I had never fully discovered.

As part of the educational system, every child attended the Coptic church service. Because I was a certified deacon, I taught Bible to the children and was well-known by the whole school for my knowledge of Scripture and my passion for teaching it. These credentials and my past performance earned me selection as the Sixth Grade Class Monitor the following year.

Although Menalu was raised with a strict Jewish background, she attended church as well, every morning and every night, just like the rest of us. She, like the other Jewish students, did not want anyone in school to know that she was Jewish because nearly all were Coptic Christians, though a few were Muslim. At the church, she was introduced to *Yesus Kristos* (Jesus Christ). Hear her story:

> *I was very interested in this God Yesus Kristos. When my father discovered that I was going to church, he was very upset. Since my family was Jewish, they really disliked Yesus. I wanted to know why they disliked him. Why was the synagogue different from the church? Why were they separate?*
>
> *I remember noticing Kokeb when he was the Sixth Grade Class Monitor. He seemed much more mature than the other boys, and I knew he was involved in the church as a deacon. There was a certain passion to the way he taught the Scriptures. For those reasons, I always wanted to meet him and felt I could learn a lot from him.*

We did meet and developed a very strong friendship,

but we never really thought romantically about each other. Everyone thought that we were siblings, so a number of men came to me, asking for my permission to marry her. Since I never thought about marrying her myself, I was not bothered by their requests. Menalu, however, was a very religious girl, and she was not interested in marrying anyone. Although many times I encouraged her to marry, her answer was always no. There was something else that helped in our developing a friendship. You see, I discovered early that Menalu was much smarter than I was. She was always being recognized for her academic achievements. Because of her, I avoided many "whippings," for I must admit that she sometimes helped me with my homework. One of her strongest subjects was history, that being my weakest. It always seemed that I sat behind her during exams. It was difficult to fight off the temptation to crane my neck to see the paper that she had adjusted for my vision alone.

Between helping my uncle, being the classroom monitor, and keeping up my studies, I was very busy. I knew I wanted to do my best for God, and I also knew that I would have to take the *Beherawi Fetana,* the National Exam, in June. This exam determined whether I would graduate from elementary school and progress to middle school into the seventh grade. It would also determine my future because The Central Education Administration targeted only the smartest children for college. Going into the exam, both Menalu and I felt confident about our passing it as we had worked very hard. The tests were sent from Gondar to the capital city of Addis Ababa to be scored. Then we had to wait two months, until September, to get the results. Some of our friends spent sleepless nights agonizing over their test results. When we were around them we experienced a little of their anxiety.

Ethiopia is considered the country of thirteen months of sunshine. Each of our months is made of thirty days. So at the end of our calendar, there are five days between the end of the year in August and the beginning of the new year in September. We call it *pagumie*. For the orthodox, this is a time of ardent fasting and prayer, a time for cleaning houses and cleansing souls.

After *pagumie* came September, which was not only significant to the students and their families because of the results of *Beherawi Fetana*, but also, the month brought with it the beautiful *adey ababa,* the yellow flower. Its tall stem and sunburst petals grew wildly all over Gondar in flower pots, flower beds, and roadsides. Everyone knew that when Ethiopia was painted yellow, it was also time for *Enkutatash,* the "gift of jewels." It is the Ethiopian New Year celebrated on September 11 at the end of the rainy season. It commemorates the time that the Queen of Sheba returned from the court of King Solomon. He had given her many precious jewels. On New Year's Eve, the towns and villages were lit with bonfires and music. In the morning, the girls wore traditional clothing of vibrant white, red, and green, in the colors of the Ethiopian flag. They went from house to house singing in rich harmonies to rival the mixed rhythms of the day, all the sounds that reflected the excitement of this event. On a piece of paper, the children drew the *adey ababa*, the yellow flower, or they would pick them and give them to neighbors in exchange for gifts.

That evening the boys did the same, dressed in the colors of Ethiopia. The *kebero*, a large drum made from a hollowed-out log with hides stretched around each end, marked out the cadence of the boys' chants. Like the girls, they received gifts as they went from house to house giving away the *adey ababa* in celebration of a new year. In the homes of the affluent, lamb was served and in the other homes, chickens were roasted for a sumptuous feast.

Finally, the day came when the results of the *Beherawi Fetana* were posted at the school. Parents and children filed up to the lists taped to the windows where students were identified by numbers and not names. The screams of joy that burst forth from those who had passed the test were punctuated by the tears and sobs of those who had failed. Menalu and I were nervous as we approached the window, but reasonably sure that sounds of joy would flow from our lips. I must reiterate we had worked hard. Usually, if a student passes, he or she gets new clothes, and the family celebrates by killing a lamb. That evening, Menalu and I were wearing new clothes and eating tender roasted lamb. Hallelujah!

Seventh grade brought with it some important changes to my life. First of all, there was only one middle school in

Gondar, so students, whom I had never met before, attended from various elementary schools. Although I saw Menalu during the day, I was not in any of her classes. Menalu met Dejetnu; her name means "people will follow you." She was much older than we were. She was already married to a priest and had two children. Because the Dergue government had issued a decree that everyone would be educated and no one would any longer sign their names with a seal, Dejetnu had to return to school. Menalu and I were able to continue our friendship through attending church. Gondar abounded with forty-four Orthodox churches and the church calendar was replete with a holy day for every day of the year. I served as a deacon in Gabriel Church, but we visited a different church every day. Most of our time was spent at *Medehane Alem Church* (Saviour of the World) where we were part of the *Haymanote Abew* (the Faith of our Fathers), a Youth Group/ Bible Study Program. We studied the Bible and sang songs in Amharic. It was completely run by young people between the ages of eighteen and thirty; we never saw any adults while we were there.

Chapter 10

Gondar—Fasilades High School

In eighth grade, Menalu and I were reunited in a classroom setting. This time there were three of us: Menalu, Dejetnu, and me. When I was in eighth grade, the *ferenge* for whom Rekebenaha worked completed his assignment in Ethiopia and returned to Canada. She found a job as a teacher in an international school in Gondar, rented a house, and asked me to live with her. I must admit that I would have never made it to the eighth grade or even to adulthood today had it not been for the support and encouragement from Rekebenaha. When my aunt and uncle worked me unbelievably hard, it was her voice telling me I could make it and not to give up. With her support, Menalu, Dejetnu, and I worked doggedly to prepare for the eighth grade *Beherawi Fatana*. All three of us saw God's hand on our lives as He gave us continual favor in our friendship and academic studies.

In ninth grade, the student body became more diversified as the high school drew from other areas. It was at this time that we had to select a course of study: Productive Technology or Commerce. I chose the highly competitive area of Productive Technology studies. My class was composed of mostly boys, thirty of the best students in our district. Menalu and Dejetnu selected Commerce. This crowded discipline was comprised of eighty to ninety students. There were not enough desks for everyone, so if someone arrived late, he or she had to sit on the floor.

In this grade I was elected to be Chairman of High School Students. As a result, I was given more access to teachers and more freedom to punish misbehaving students. The Communist government had passed rules that students had to wear khaki uniforms, and the girls could not wear jewelry or high-heeled shoes. For breaking any one of these rules, I meted out the punishment. Sometimes I confiscated women's jewelry or shoes and locked them up. If they wanted to recover their belongings, I made them pay a fine. Most students were afraid of me. Oftentimes, the girls tried to seduce me to get special privileges or obtain their belongings, but I had no interest in girls. Such disinterest was the result of my orthodox upbringing, which guided my life and my choices until I married.

That time would come sooner than I thought. The school officials chose ten students from every province who had excelled academically in grades nine and ten. I had the fourth highest grade point average in my class, so I was one of those selected to attend the Technical School in the capital city of Addis Ababa. There would be no room and board and no meals. If students were to attend the school, they must have support from their families. Fortunately, my maternal great grandmother's sister lived in Addis Ababa. She had agreed to help me with room and board. Rekebenaha would help with meals and living expenses. God had opened more doors for me and given me another chance to excel. There was, however, one area of my life that I needed to address.

Menalu had turned down marriage to everyone who approached her. I was becoming increasingly aware that my childhood friend was the one I wanted to marry. Could God have been preserving her for me? Did we not enjoy going to church together, serving the Lord together, laughing together? Didn't she know more about me than anyone else?

"Menalu, I have nothing," I told her. "No money, no job, no home. But I promise to work hard so that I can have all of those things and provide for you. Next year, I will be going to Technical School. Will you wait for me and marry me?"

"There is something I must tell you, Kokeb. I have kept it a secret from you, but if we are to be married, I cannot hide it any longer."

"You can tell me anything, and it won't change the way I feel about you. I love you," I told her.

"I am Jewish. My father is Jewish. He keeps the

Sabbath and the *Kashrut* laws."

"I believe that I am Jewish, too," I said. "My father always told me that we are the children of *Wolte Yisrael* [Mother Israel]." We were both very excited.

"Our marriage will be a covenant that you and I make with God based upon truth," she said. "So, Kokeb, out marriage is not dependent on whether you go to Technical School or not. I am not looking for material things. I want to make a life together with you. So yes, I will wait for you."

I was so motivated to work hard. Menalu deserved so much and I wanted to give it to her. As the time came closer to leave for the capital city, I had nothing to give to my future wife but a vow. I took her to the Ethiopian Coptic Church, one of the oldest churches in Gondar. Made of stone, the place was bathed in a solemn silence that showered us both. It seemed to sanction what we were about to do. Pictures of angels and saints hung on every wall. They watched us enter, and they would watch as we made our vows.

Their eyes followed as we walked to the front, where there was a Holy Bible. We stood in front of the Holy of Holies, placed our hands upon the Bible, and declared our commitment to one another. I pledged first:

"Menalu, I promise before the God of Israel that I will be true to you and work hard to support you. In this life nothing will separate us, not sickness, or health—only death. If we part for any other reason, God Himself will punish me."

"Kokeb, I promise to wait for you and be the faithful,

supportive wife that you need."

The saints and angels had listened to us, so we were sure that the God of Israel heard us. I had felt His favor upon me for as long as I could remember. Every mile I had traveled and every heartache I had experienced had led me to this one moment where I had found fulfillment.

After we recited our vows, life continued as normal. Each of us lived with relatives, so we had no time or place to be together. Even if we had, we knew that we could not consummate our marriage because our ceremony was unofficial. I was a deacon and Menalu a godly woman. I respected my wife, she respected my position, and we both honored God. Sometimes we would steal away to the church to pray, so that we could spend some time together, but we never violated the sacredness of the building.

Three months later, I told the priest what we had done.

"You are a *kohen,* Kokeb," the priest said. "In the orthodox church, your marriage must be expressed officially in a holy ceremony. You must wear special clothes and a crown. You must give your wife a ring and it must be done in front of witnesses."

We knew our parents would not approve, so we kept it a secret from them. We invited about ten of our friends to stand as witnesses of the heartfelt vows, now official, that we had spoken in front of each other, the angels, and God.

I wore a crown topped with a cross and framed with silver fringe that rested just above my eyelids. They draped me in a robe that shimmered under the lights of the building. In my hand I carried a five-foot staff topped with a large cross, adorned with a long striped red and white sash. Menalu wore the feminine version of the crown with a brim that rested over her eyes. Sashes billowed from the crown she tied under her chin. The women had clothed her in a burgundy robe. In my heart, I had known that she was a queen, and now she was dressed like one, bedecked in royal attire just for me. The priest led us in the vows that we had recited to each other several months ago.

On August 21, 1983 Menalu and I were husband and wife. Our friend Dejetnu and her husband prepared the food for our reception. When our parents discovered the marriage, they felt we had dishonored and disrespected them. It would be three years before Menalu's father would finally bless her and accept me as his son-in-law.

We did not take the time to consummate our marriage after this ceremony either. I left Menalu shortly afterwards with the memory of a marriage, but not one of fully becoming her husband. The nature of my departure made the one-and-a-half day bus ride to Addis Ababa very difficult. I was married now, so I could not think of only myself. Menalu was now my chief concern. I wrestled with these strong first-felt emotions.

Chapter 11

Addis Ababa—Technical School, 1984

AFTER THREE DAYS OF GETTING ADJUSTED TO THE CITY, I HAD TO GET up very early to travel an hour by bus to school. Living with my great-aunt meant more restrictions because I was boarding at her home. Every day I anxiously looked for money from my sister Rekebenaha, but sometimes it did not come. I wrote Menalu every day, and although I was soothed by her letters, they always aroused within me a desire to be with her. I studied hard, not just to excel and to provide a home for my wife, but to take my mind off my hunger. My stomach played call-and-response with my mind. It growled and my mouth said, "I am hungry."

Adding to my personal problems, the Communist government arrested or killed young people they thought were sympathetic to the rebels. I had found a Coptic church in Addis Ababa, but worshipping there did not seem to lift my depression. I went through the motions of speaking lifeless words from a lifeless heart. I wanted to eat. I wanted a place of my own. I wanted Menalu. By the sixth month, I was thoroughly depressed.

Then I met him—Messay. He walked into the classroom —no, he sauntered. He seemed almost carefree. There did not seem to be a single weight of life that he was carrying upon his shoulders. I think I was carrying his and mine, too. His speech was full of life and zest. Either I could resent him or I could befriend him and find out about the source of his joy.

"Why are you always happy?" I managed to ask one day.

"Ahhh, Kokeb, you can have this joy, too."

"How?" I asked cautiously. "Chat?" (a green leaf used as a drug)

"Let me take you there, my friend," he said. Boy, was it enticing! "Let me take you to a place where you can get joy."

"Where is it?" I asked with reservation.

"You want to come? Then come. I will take you to the place tonight. We will go together," he smiled.

All evening I thought about where Messay would take me. Would it be a place where young boys go and experiment with girls? Would it be a cult? Would it be the lady in the marketplace who swore that her elixir would change my life? Or could it be a church?

I met Messay just as I said I would, and there he was,

greeting me with the biggest smile, the warmest hand on my shoulder. "Come on, brother, let's find you joy!" he said.

We stood outside the Lutheran Church, Ledeta Mekale Yesus. It was the only church in the area that had not been forcibly closed by the Dergue Communist regime. It was the hub of humanitarian aid, hospitals, and schools during the communist takeover. Different organizations came to hold its meetings there.

"I don't know, Messay. I don't know if this is for me," I said, remembering all the priestly warnings.

"What do you have to lose?" he asked.

I had nothing to lose. No one need know that I ever set foot inside a Pentecostal assembly.

I had heard stories about Charismatic/Pentecostal meetings—the exuberant shouting, the quaking and quivering bodies, people falling to the floor or frothing at the mouth—and I had been told by every religious figure I knew to "stay away from those places!" No one could have told me that I would be standing in front of, let alone entering, such a congregation—not even out of utter curiosity. I was there because my new best friend said it contained the source of my much-needed joy.

We walked into an auditorium filled with over 500 souls. True to all the stories, people were standing, clapping wildly, dancing frenetically. The atmosphere was like the rush of the falls from the Blue Nile, heaving and alive. We were ushered to empty seats in the midst of people who smiled at us as they made way for our entrance. A choir in color-coordinated robes sang a song that could pierce the shell of the hardest of men. There was life in their music, a depth to their joy, and seemingly no limit to their passion. To this day I have no idea of the name of the song; all I know is that unheeded tears were streaming down my face.

Attending nightly prayer meetings with my father had not moved me this way. Kissing the Bishop's ring and becoming a deacon had not stirred my soul so deeply. Compared to this experience, walking into the Holy of Holies was like the third cup of coffee in a *bunna* (coffee) ceremony; this had to be the first! I wept, though, not out of sorrow, and when I did, the weights lifted. This must be the joy of which Messay had spoken! This must be what changed his life!

Then the preacher came out and talked about *Yesus Kristos*. His voice rose and fell, not in rehearsed liturgy, but like a man who knew that he had found the only piece of bread left and was beseeching you not to search any further, but to share it with him. He spoke of how Pilate had brought *Yesus Kristos* before the crowd and asked, "'What should I do with *Yesus Kristos*?' And *Yesus* asks the same of you today. What will you do with Him? Will you reject Him? Will you crucify Him? Or will you receive Him? He is the One who died for you? He is the One who bore your sins. Some of you might be saying, 'I don't need Him.' I declare to you tonight that He is the only source of life, of peace, of JOY!" I couldn't believe it! He said, 'joy!' That's what I wanted! That's what Messay had! That's what Messay said I needed. The preacher explained the whole process of receiving Him. I did not want to search any longer. I wanted to partake of this sole piece of bread that the preacher had found and was offering to me.

"Who will say, 'I need *Yesus Kristos*'? Who will receive Him tonight?" he compelled.

Before I knew it, I was standing down front. Nothing else was important in that moment. I did not remember Messay. I did not remember Menalu. This moment was so monumental that I did not want it to cease. I took the bread and gobbled it like the starving, ravenous man I was. I could not stop eating of this Bread of Life. All depression departed. How can depression live where there is absolute joy? How can death exist in the midst of life?

Even though I had reservations about this "salvation process," I had to receive all of Him when I was confronted with the truth which exposed all the things that I was feeling at the time. I had no doubt that my Orthodox Jewish wife who worshiped as a Coptic Christian would do the same—accept the whole truth of *Yesus Kristos*.

I went back to my life. My conditions had not changed. I was still living with my great aunt. I was still hungry. I still missed Menalu. But I had changed. I did not let these adverse situations cripple me and change my outlook. There was something within me that was in control of my perspective. I was in control of the impact of my circumstances upon my life. Menalu must know as soon as possible! I could tell that my letters, teeming with life, with hope, with boundless joy, were confusing to Menalu. In her letters she begged me not to change. She reminded me of how we felt about the Pentecostal churches and all the cautions to stay away from them.

"When school closes in the winter," I wrote to her, "I will come to Gondar. I will tell you everything. I know that you are afraid of making wrong decisions. But I assure you, we will not make any mistakes about God."

In the meantime, I attended underground Bible studies. They were held in the homes of believers, but getting there was all very secretive. It took an hour to ninety minutes to travel by bus to the homes. If we went as a group, we would have to wait in fifteen-minute intervals to enter the house so that we did not arouse suspicion. Sometimes others would arrive three hours before the study started so that they could avoid the vigilant eyes of the Dergue soldiers. Many of the believers had been jailed, beaten, and even maimed, but it was a fate we risked so that we could find hope in a hopeless era.

Before my experience at Ledeta Mekale Yesus Church, I had considered *Yesus Kristos* to be like one of the angels, or one of the saints that hung on the walls of the Coptic churches. I had never considered him as my personal Savior. Now I walked with Him daily. I talked with Him. He was my Friend. I learned about the power and Person of the Holy Spirit. I saw miracles happen before my eyes when we prayed in the name of *Yesus*. I saw lives changed; mine was the greatest example for me. When I married Menalu, I thought that the God of

Israel had preserved me for that moment, but now I realized that *this* was the moment—knowing the One about whom I had preached since I was ten, and loving and drawing near to the One who lived in the Holy of Holies, a place that I could have never entered alone. Now I could live in the Holy of Holies every day! I could not wait for Menalu to hear the truth from my lips!

When we were in school, she was drawn to me because I was mature and spiritual. I wanted her to know that I was still mature and even more spiritual. "*Yesus*, Holy Spirit of God, please reveal to Menalu the truth of who You are," I prayed in the way I had learned from my new experience.

Winter arrived and I was home with Menalu. I had missed her so much. I told her about my experience with *Yesus Kristos* again. This time she could look into my eyes and see that I was not deluded.

I shared with her the truth of the Scriptures as it had been shared with me:

John 14:6 :

> *"Jesus answered, 'I am the way and the truth and the life. No one comes to the Father except through me.'"*

We had been trying to gain access to the Father through saints and liturgy, through rituals and rites. *Yesus Kristos* was the ***only*** access.

Jeremiah 31:31:

> *"The time is coming," declares the LORD, "when I will make a new covenant with the house of Israel and with the house of Judah."*

God had said He was going to make a new covenant with us,

where he would write his laws upon our hearts. I understood it now, and I wanted so desperately for Menalu to understand also.

I Timothy 2:5:

> *"For there is one God and one mediator between God and men, the man Christ Jesus, who gave himself as a ransom for all men—the testimony given in its proper time."*

Yesus is the Mediator. Not the *qess*! Not the bishop! We had been looking toward man for too long.

Acts 4:12:

> *"Salvation is found in no one else, for there is no other name under heaven given to men by which we must be saved."*

Here was the clincher! Being saved! Knowing *Yesus* as the Savior. "It is by His Name and His Name alone, Menalu, that we will be saved."

After a week of talking and praying and reasoning with the Scriptures, Menalu accepted *Yesus Kristos* as her personal Savior. We began our walk with *Yesus* together, as man and wife. This time when I took her in my arms, I was filled with a new passion and deeper love for her. We both wanted *Yesus Kristos,* not just the idea of Him, but a relationship with Him. Such a desire enhanced our personal intimacy with one another. This began a new chapter in our lives, actually, the most difficult part of our journey, but *Yesus* would be with us.

Chapter 12

Addis Ababa & Wonja Showa—The Sugar Factory

I RETURNED TO ADDIS ABABA TO FINISH MY EDUCATION AT THE Technical School. At the end of the year I received my diploma, certification as a machinist. Menalu finished in her Commerce School education. We continued to keep in touch through our letters and to grow in our relationship with *Yesus Kristos*. That year Menalu passed the National Exam for college and therefore had the freedom to move about. I found a room in Addis, and Menalu and I had our first home together. It was only ten minutes' walking distance from the Technical School.

Although Menalu attended church with me, she was frightened at every turn. She did not want anyone to know that we were Christians, let alone Jews. In addition to *hearing* horror stories of the arrests and assaults by Dergue soldiers, she had *seen* them occur as well. Her fears were layered with further rejection and alienation; neither of our families wanted anything to do with us since we had accepted *Yesus Kristos*. We did not know how to convince them that we had not betrayed them, nor had we been brainwashed. Our letters to them went unanswered. We had no one else but each other and the God we served. Through this solitary period in our lives, we learned that God gives special grace for special situations. That's what He did for us. We did not crumble or sink into abject depression. We trusted God. We were living Psalm 24:1-6:

The earth is the LORD's, and everything in it,
the world, and all who live in it;
for he founded it upon the seas
and established it upon the waters.
Who may ascend the hill of the LORD ?
Who may stand in his holy place?
He who has clean hands and a pure heart,
who does not lift up his soul to an idol
or swear by what is false.
He will receive blessing from the LORD
and vindication from God his Savior.
Such is the generation of those who seek him,
who seek your face, O God of Jacob.

Everything belonged to the Lord, and as long as we remained faithful to Him, He would vindicate us in the midst of our families and against all our enemies.

The next year I completed my education at the Technical School, but I had no choice as to where I would work. The Dergue government determined that for me. I was employed as a machinist in a Communist-run bullet factory. I had a government ID from them that identified me as a number, *their* worker to assist them in developing bullets and bombs used to kill *my* people who opposed a government bent on controlling or destroying all those who resisted their methods. The company was leery of people stealing bullets and possibly selling them to the enemy, so security was very tight. Soldiers were stationed at every door of every building. They were even positioned on the roofs. When we left the premises, we passed through several checkpoints. Whenever I walked into any room in the plant, the soldiers searched me. No part of the body or piece of clothing was off limits to them.

I worked there for five months. If I worked one more month, I would not be able to get another job, nor would I have the right to challenge any of their decisions about my employment. I would be solely and absolutely *theirs*. Therefore, I had to find a way out…*soon*. I knew that the God of Israel had protected and provided for me all my life. He is the One who gave me miracle after miracle. And then, I had not really *known* Him, not like I knew Him now through His Son *Yesus Kristos* and through the Holy Spirit. Surely He would provide another much-needed miracle.

I had a friend who worked in the Labor Department in

Addis Ababa. She had grown up in Gondar with me, and we attended the same church. ID cards were given only to those who were looking for work. I went to her to get an ID so that I could secretly get a new job. She issued me one. I found out that a sugar factory in Wonja Showa in the town of Nazret, about 100 miles from Addis, was looking for three machinists.

That was my trade! Maybe this was the miracle that I was seeking. To get there required a half day's travel by public transportation. In November, I went there, applied, and was accepted the same day. I would start in December.

Menalu wanted to live with me, even though Wonja Showa would take her away from a bustling city to a place where sugar cane grew more plentiful than people. Along the highway leading to our new home, sugar cane stood like rows of soldiers standing at attention for miles, their leafy arms waving the onlooker onward. The area seemed desolate, apart from these silent sentinels. They knew not how to be friends or to console. They simply waved us on.

In my new job, I was given a one-bedroom single home with a living room, a kitchen, and a bathroom. I also had a salary and freedom. In Wonja Showa, Menalu and I were separated from all that was familiar. This would be the honeymoon that Menalu and I never had, an opportunity to start a sweet, new life together in a town of sugar cane.

The work was better, but very challenging! The job started in the cane fields with the outside workers. Using sharp machetes and knives, they cut the thick, jointed stalks near the ground, making sure that the roots remained for the new growth. Workers fed the canes into a press so that the sweet fluid was squeezed out of them. In another machine, through the process of evaporation, the fluid was cleansed of the impurities from the crushed stalk.

We produced the parts that would run the machines in this sweatshop of a factory. We brought the metals and materials, the blueprints, and the manuals to create machine parts, adjust gears for efficiency, and troubleshoot whenever a problem arose. If we broke anything or caused the malfunctioning of any machine, the cost was deducted from our salary, so I was very careful. There were three shifts and everyone had to rotate weekly: 7:00 a.m. to 3:00 p.m., 3:00 p.m. to 11:00 p.m., and 11:00 p.m. to 7:00 a.m. The latter was the most difficult and every three weeks, I worked that shift.

That third week was especially difficult for Menalu. She was home alone in a strange place. During that time, she prepared my meals, kept house, and tried to learn the native language of the area—Orominga, spoken by the Oromos, a completely different language from Amharic. All the machinist's manuals were in English, so I did not have a problem communicating on my job. She also worried about raising a family in Wonja Showa. The water was full of rust and other impurities that turned the children's teeth brown. Malaria was rampant. These were just a few reasons why we would not make this city our home.

Wonja Showa was also Addis Ababa in miniature. The

Dergue soldiers were everywhere. We could not freely practice our faith for fear of being discovered and "dealt with." Menalu and I would pray together, but we did not have a place to worship or a community of believers to talk with about our faith. We were like little people living in a miniature house with soldiers peering through our open windows, scrutinizing our every move. We had to look beyond those intrusive eyes to know that there was One with greater sight Who was watching them watch us. We believed He would not allow us to be harmed.

Chapter 13

Wonja Showa—1985

ANIMALS CAN SENSE DISASTER LONG BEFORE HUMANS. BIRDS WILL take flight before a drought comes. At the slightest scent of smoke, land animals will scurry from the troubled area.

Like disaster, drought, and smoke, the Communists had already encroached upon our lives and our freedom. They were entrenched now. Everywhere you looked or went they were there, like a memory you couldn't get rid of or a dream that plagued you every time you closed your eyes.

Fear lurked around every corner. It whispered in your ear and crawled into your mouth, its poisonous taste refusing to be diluted no matter how much one prays or believes. Everyone was fearful.

The arrests had not stopped. The beatings were more frequent, not necessarily because someone broke their law, but because they needed amusement, and sought to display their power by making daily examples of any who wanted to defect. But we knew a Higher Power, the One Who sustained us.

Unlike the animals, some of us never had a chance to run, not sensing the danger until it was in our faces. Some saw it and were paralyzed by it. Some tried not to upset the status quo and conformed to the dangerous presence. That's what Menalu and I did until we realized that fear was stealing our hope and crushing our faith.

Then we heard of those who had already taken flight and begun to scurry. When we first heard of Operation Moses, I was living in Addis Ababa and Menalu in Gondar. Many Ethiopians considered it just a rumor about the *Beta Yisrael* (Black Jews) being airlifted out of Sudan and taken to Israel. It sounded like a children's tale with no substance. Maybe it was just a tale that brought hope of survival for those whose family members had not been heard from again after their trek into Sudan. Maybe it was just the result of the Jewish dream to escape persecution and live in the land that had been promised to them. Since Gondar is on the Sudanese border, Menalu had more accurate information.

One day in Wonja Showa changed our lives forever. We received a letter from a childhood friend who was now living in Israel. He spoke of Operation Moses, how he and some others were airlifted out of Sudan. We could not believe that substance was being added to the rumor. He encouraged us to get to Sudan. "There," he said, "an airplane will pick you up and bring you here, to the Promised Land."

The children's tale had morphed into reality. It was true! It was there in black and white. Truth etched onto a piece of paper, spoken by a man, not a boy, shared by an adult, not a child. Was this the answer for us? Ethiopia was our home, but it was not a refuge. The Communists had come, turning our home into a fright zone. Any place would be better than this, especially the Promised Land. And, Menalu's father Melesse had always encouraged her to go to Israel; he had always believed that she would pave the way for him to go. We made our decision. We both wanted to go. Now, all we had to do was develop a strategy to accomplish our goal.

We forged a letter from her father saying that he was sick and needed to see his daughter before he died. We knew this was not far from the truth because Melesse was older then and ill. After working ten months at the sugar factory, I sent Menalu to Gondar. Once in Gondar, Menalu would travel to Metema, where she, her mother, and sister had narrowly escaped the Dergue soldiers and where Melesse was well known by the townspeople and by the rebels.

Her uncle helped her to get into Tumet, a half-day walk from Metema. It was a town controlled by rebel forces—the last bastion before the border of Sudan. It had been two years since Menalu had seen her family. Melesse had left Metema and retired in this quiet little town. Because he owned considerable livestock, Tumet was a place where his cattle could roam on verdant plains, eating rich grasses. He could practice Orthodox Judaism without fear of persecution, and like the patriarch Abraham, Melesse ascended a nearby mountain where he worshipped the God of Israel. Tumet was the place where he could keep the Sabbath and *Kashrut* according to the letter of the law.

After two months in Tumet, Menalu sent me a letter saying she was sick. She wanted me to come. I asked my boss for permission to see her. After working a full year, I knew I could receive a two-week vacation.

"You can't go to Gondar Province. It is a dangerous place," he counseled. "Don't you know that there is war between the government and the rebel fighters?"

"I know that Metema is a dangerous place," I retorted, "but it is very important that I get there to see her." Metema was part of the Gondar Province.

"You know that there is a chance that you may not return," he said rhetorically, trying to convince me not to go.

"My wife is ill. That is a risk I have to take," I concluded. He gave me permission to go to Gondar. I had two weeks.

Part II of our plan was underway.

Part III

Beyond Imagination...

Chapter 14

Wonja Showa to Metema

LEAVING WONJA SHOWA WAS THE SIMPLEST LEG OF MY TRIP. I PAID the fare and boarded a bus that took me to Addis Ababa. A day-and-a-half travel took me past the Showa Province, the Nile River, and into Gojam Province. I traversed narrow mountain roads with steep cliffs and sharp drops. Sometimes drivers would misjudge a turn, grinding their brakes on downhill slopes and be forced to choose between running off a cliff or running into the mountain. When they had the mental acuity and time to make a choice, they always chose the latter.

As we passed through Debre Markos in the Gojam Province, I remembered my journey there as a boy of twelve. That was so long ago and many religious experiences later. We went into Fenote Selam (which means 'The Light of Peace') and spent the night. Our driver instructed us to stay in a hotel but to be prepared for his departure at 6:00 a.m. He warned that he would be leaving at 6:00 sharp. My fellow passengers and I made sure we lodged in the hotels nearest the bus station. At 5:30 a.m, we heard the driver blowing the horn, giving us the last warning. We scrambled to our feet and were out the door.

We had lunch in Bahar Dar, and I remembered my first visit there, when I had met *ferenge-och* who blessed me so that I could find Rekebenaha. I tried to sit back and relax, but I could not. I was concerned about the next leg of my trip before meeting up with Menalu. We arrived at 4:00 p.m. in Gondar. This was the place of my adolescence and the home of my sister, Rekebenaha. My every intention was to avoid her. She was now part of the Dergue Communist Party, working full-time as the leader of the Women's Association. I knew that she would not be sympathetic to my cause. However, I also knew that my presence in town would not go unnoticed, especially since I had to stay several days to secure all the resources needed for my travels. There were too many people who knew me. So I decided just to go to her directly.

I went to her house, but she was not there. The house servants and neighbors were surprised by my visit. Usually it is customary for visitors to give advance warning so that the necessary preparations can be made. This was not the kind of visit that I had intended; actually, I had not intended a visit at all. The servants promptly called her to let her know I was there. She was amazed. She cancelled her meetings and quickly came home. She was very curious about what was going on. All she knew about my life was that I was working in Wonja Showa at the Sugar Factory.

"Kokeb, what are you doing here? What's going on?" my sister asked.

"Menalu is in Tumet, sick. I have to get to her. I cannot leave her there alone," I said.

"But, Kokeb, you cannot go there! It is too dangerous," she protested.

"Do you expect me to leave her there alone? I am her husband. This is what I promised—to protect her, and that's what I am going to do."

"Kokeb, do not do anything crazy," she said.

It was better that Rekebenaha did not know the truth. I knew she would rather that I be arrested by the Dergue regime than to risk death on my way to Metema with the purpose of fleeing the country. As long as she believed I was going to help my sick wife, she would not try to stop me.

After three days, I found Dagnew; he would be my guide for a portion of my trip. He ordered me to get rid of all modern clothes and to think, dress, and act like a peasant, a farmer. So I bought shorts and *gabi,* worn by Ethiopian peasants. I donned a turban and held a shepherd's stick in my hand. I was ready to join Menalu.

He addressed me and others who were taking the same trip: "There are guides waiting to take you to different locations throughout your journey to Metema. We are like a chain. I am the first link in that chain. You must do as I say, and you must follow me."

From Gondar at Arada Station we paid the fare and boarded the last minibus at 9:00 p.m. headed for Azezo, the location of the Gondar airport. He drove around the outskirts of the town taking us in the direction of Azezo. We took the last drop off before entering the city. We would not go into the town because it was completely controlled by Dergue. From there we walked to the designated place where Dagnew said he would meet us. After meeting with him, we divided into two groups. The first group went with him; the second group, the one I was in, followed as if not to be acquainted with the first. For an hour we walked this way and then finally we were able to walk together as one group.

We started going toward Chilga, a small city in Gondar Province about twenty-five miles from Azezo. Usually to travel to Chilga by bus would take a half-day but not for the route we needed to take. We used forest paths and mountain trails.

Some got very sick from exposure to the elements and walking over difficult terrain. Greater than sickness and hunger, however, was the threat of rebel groups who would extinguish us more quickly than illness or famine ever could. We walked until early morning and found a cave where we could rest and shield ourselves from the elements. I had not walked as much since I was a teenager. Now, when I look back on those times, I know that the grace of God was upon my life. I found some sugar in my pocket. I put it in my mouth and poured water in after it. The sweetness revived me and took my mind off the perils of the journey.

The following night we arrived at the next meeting point just outside of Chilga. Dagnew connected us with Addisu, the next link in the chain; unlike Dagnew, Addisu carried a gun. I could only surmise that this leg of the journey was much riskier. It was true. He took us fifty miles from outside the Chilga area, around the mountainous region of Negade Baher. At night, under a shroud of intense darkness, we hid from the soldiers. The landscape was littered with the bodies of my comrades who had attempted to do what I was now doing—escape. Some bodies had been mutilated by wild animals; others were desperately waiting for final rites, slowly decomposing with every climate change. I knew that I could have been one of those bodies, and Menalu could have been one of the unfortunate victims of rape, robbery, or murder. But the God of Israel afforded us another miracle—miracle after miracle through his limitless grace and for His divine purpose. More than 4,000 Jewish people died of starvation and malaria or were killed trying to escape Ethiopia during that time.

We could hear the mating calls of baboons who live in the mountains and see the ibexes, swift mountain goats with their fantastic spiraled horns, nimbly scaling the rocky peaks. Wolves and birds of prey scoured the land and the sky in search of the wounded, weak, slow or unlucky.

Some of us were discouraged and tried to discourage others. I thought of the Israelites when they had just come out of Egypt (Exodus 14). They tried to discourage each other and

Moses from venturing any further. They wanted to return to Egypt. They said that life in Egypt was much better than life in the wilderness. I tried to see the greater reality. I tried to see what Moses saw as he forged ahead. Even though I could understand the Israelites' perspective, I had come too far to turn back. Moses was my example.

In ten days we arrived in Kokeit and spent two days there to rest. Addisu handed us over to the third link in the chain, Maru, our new guide. Our journey with him took us over surmountable hills and barren flatlands, through plush valleys and craggy highlands. We crossed shallow streams whose waters we readily used for drinking, washing or bathing. We had to be careful because wild animals, like tigers, came to drink from the small streams. I had heard of many tales of people being attacked by wild animals, who like us, had come only to refresh themselves. He took us through the Mekar Forests, whose trees are used to make *etan*, incense. I breathed deeply as I felt I was walking through God's own aromatic garden. Any moment I imagined I'd see the Mighty One basking in the heavenly fragrance that He created.

Eventually, we came out of the mountains and there were the valleys in front of us, stretching out for miles, like patchwork cloth unfurled before us. We breathed in hope and exhaled despair. We arrived at Atbara Wonz (Atbara River). At this point, our morale was truly lifted; we were more hopeful. There is something about running water that pours life into people. No wonder the Holy Spirit is symbolized by moving, gushing, flowing water. The river was our lifeline, so we followed its sinuous path wherever it wandered.

Finally, after twelve days, we had arrived in Metema! I was weary from the journey and all that I had seen, but galvanized by the refreshing thought of seeing Menalu again.

But I still needed a way to get into Tumet. I knew that if the Communists discovered that I was going to Tumet to get to Sudan, I would be killed and it would be weeks, years, or even *never* before Menalu discovered that I was dead. I was in a very tricky position. If Dergue soldiers found out I was going to Sudan, they would think I was going just to join the rebel forces, and if the rebels found out, they might think I was spying for Dergue. I needed God's help!

The government of Metema allowed certain people to go to Sudan for trade, so I joined up with four others who had a similar mission and we pretended to be merchants. We found a merchant who had a donkey and asked if we could travel with him. There was a trade route that merchants take, so in that sense the journey was not clandestine. I had learned that even some of the merchants were spies for the Dergue, so I had to be careful. I could not share any more information than was necessary. To further hamper communication during our travels, the dialect and accent of merchants from Metema were so different from mine.

Every minute we thanked the Lord for the moon. Every mountain peak looked the same as did every forest, so it would be very easy to get lost were it not for the guides sticking to well-traveled trails. There was never enough food, so the hunger that plagued me when I was in Technical School in Addis Ababa had returned. I never seemed to be a stranger to it. The cold nights set my teeth on edge. In the midst of those adversities, the guide any minute would kneel quickly at the sound of gunfire, and we had to mimic him. It was all about self-preservation. But if we died, we died...and our bodies would lie there helplessly as food for the wild animals or nutrients for the soil. There was no guarantee for our lives. All I knew was that ultimately I wanted to get to Sudan, and that trek was just the means to the end.

We journeyed in the middle of the night hiding from Communist soldiers, and one morning they greeted us with guns in our faces. It seemed like a cruel joke—the hiding, the carefulness, the inconvenience, the difficulty—only to be discovered so uneventfully. They arrested us, beat us with the butts of their rifles, and then jailed us.

I had always been bold. Like when I told my father that I wanted to attend a modern school. Like when I stood before the Bishop's assistance and said my "*Malka Yesus*"! So when I stood before the officer again, my boldness spoke.

"Sir," I said, "what can I do to convince you I am not against the government? My wife is sick in Tumet. See, this letter is from her." I showed him the letter. "My sister works for your government; she holds a high position. If I am against your government, then I am against her. I tell you that is not so; she is very precious to me."

They sentenced me to one day in prison in Metema. I remembered that there were two men like me in prison once, almost 1,500 years ago. I remembered that their only recourse was prayer and worship. God shook the foundations of their prison with an earthquake. Maybe He could do that for me. So I prayed all night like Paul and Silas. In the morning light, I knew my sentence could have been much worse.

One of the officers in the prison had grown up with me in Gondar. He told me, "You should tell your wife to meet you here, in Metema. There is no way you will be able to get to Tumet," he warned. "Find a way to get your wife here." He took my ID cards because he did not trust that I would do as he suggested. He wanted to protect himself as much as me. He warned me not to leave the city.

I found Menalu's uncle, which was very simple to accomplish in a small city. I wanted to protect his identity, so I acted as if I did not know him. After our secret meetings, Menalu's uncle took me in the middle of the night on a journey to Tumet. We traveled through forested mountains where huts were as sparse as friendly faces in this war-torn region. The only lights that guided us were those of the moon and stars dappling the expansive sky. Rebel outposts were everywhere, and our sighting of guns were as numerous as the peaks of the Simien Mountains. I was afraid of the rebels and had heard of their cruelty. My mind played soccer with my thoughts until, like the soccer ball of my childhood, they were limp rags: maybe they will not allow us to go to Sudan, maybe they will force us to fight with them, maybe, maybe, maybe. I had heard that the rebels did not want anyone to cross the border into Sudan. They wanted them to join the resistance and fight the Communists.

Because we had taken the longest route and the most secretive journey, after four days, I arrived in Tumet. I found Menalu. It had been nearly three months since I had last seen her. All I wanted to do was hold her in my arms and never let her go. We stayed on another three weeks as we had no idea if Menalu would ever see her family again, and because Melesse wanted to sell some of his cattle to cover our traveling expenses.

Part II of our plan had been accomplished. Now for the more difficult phase—getting into Sudan.

Top Left: Mo'ta—Kokeb's father, Priest Gedamu. **Top Right:** *(left to right)* Mo'ta—Kokeb's uncle Yemanebirhan, his mother Wobegieg, and his sister Rekebenaha holding his sister Assegedech. **Bottom Left:** Gondar—Kokeb's brother Libanos, a family friend, Kokeb, Rekebenaha at her engagement party. **Bottom Right:** Gondar—Kokeb, his sister Rekebenaha holding her baby Selam, her husband Tesfaye, and their daughter Hiwot.

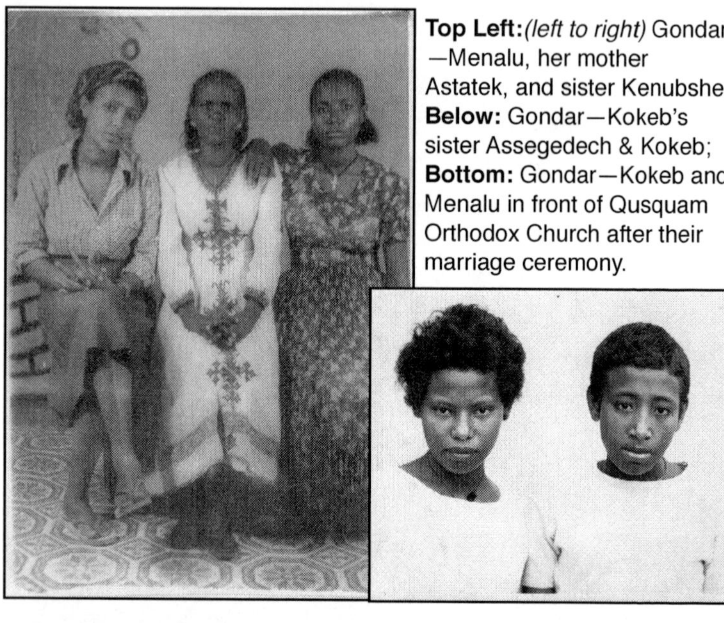

Top Left: *(left to right)* Gondar —Menalu, her mother Astatek, and sister Kenubshe; **Below:** Gondar—Kokeb's sister Assegedech & Kokeb; **Bottom:** Gondar—Kokeb and Menalu in front of Qusquam Orthodox Church after their marriage ceremony.

Top: Gondar—Aleka Tameru (Kokeb's uncle, a Coptic Orthodox priest) and Kokeb; **Bottom Left**: Sudan—Tsiehay, Menalu in Sudanese dress, and Kokeb; **Bottom Right:** Cairo, Egypt—Kokeb, dressed in Ethiopian cultural clothes, receiving gift from congregation at his ordination.

Top: Finland—Marietta, a Finnish missionary to Ethiopia, translates as Kokeb explains about the Menorah at a Lutheran Church; **Bottom**: Kokeb standing with Lutheran priests.

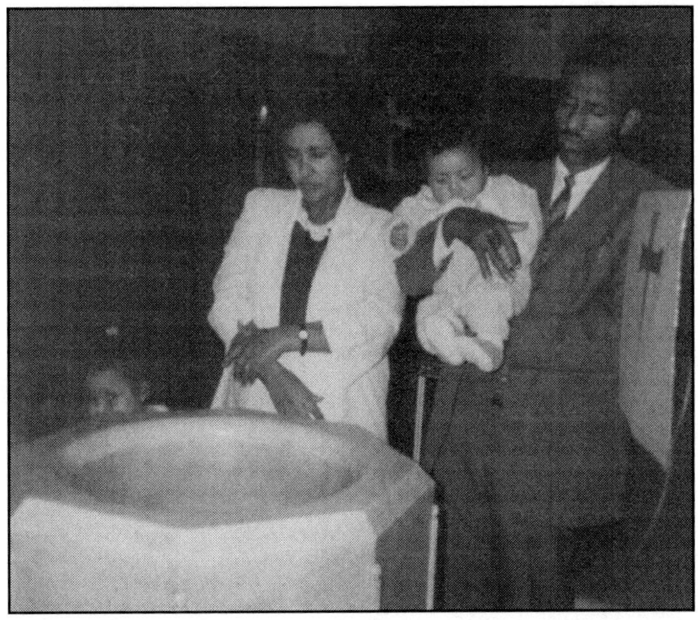

Top: Cairo,Egypt—Baby Dedication **(***Left to Right)***:** Meheret, Menalu, Ebenezer, Kokeb**. Bottom**: Galilee, Israel—*Beta Israel* Congregation, touring Cana of Galilee; Kokeb, 6th man from left on top row.

Top Left: Egypt—Kokeb standing before the pyramids. **Top Right**: Israel—Kokeb and Menalu with Jerusalem behind them. **Above**: Canada—The Gedamus at the mall, bundling up against the Canadian weather (left to right) Menalu, Ebenezer, Ruhama, Tsiona, Kokeb; **Left:** Philadelphia—The Gedamus in America *(left to right)* Ruhama, Ebenezer, Kokeb, Tsiona, Menalu.

Chapter 15

Border Crossing into Sudan—April 1987

IT WAS TIME TO LEAVE TUMET. TO SUSTAIN US DURING THE JOURNEY, we took with us *dabokolo*—like dried crackers—and the nutritious *kolo,* the seeds of wheat and sorghum. They can be stored for one to two months and are the perfect staple for traveling. We took sugar to help satisfy our hunger and sweeten the trip. Because we had been told stories about robberies, about travelers having all their money taken, we tied our money into our clothes. Our guide was a trusted kinsman of someone in our group, whose services were solicited and paid for by our families. The distance from Tumet to Sudan was not far at all, but this journey was not unlike the others. We had to take the more secretive route.

One night as we slept in the wild, we awoke to hyenas

encircling us, inching near us to sniff us and no doubt to eat us, their eyes like emeralds, glistening in the black-coffee night. "WhaaaAhhhhhh," someone screamed, awakening everyone and scattering the ravenous beasts.

We had to go through Negade Baher, the mountainous area from which I had just come, to get to Gurva. Our new guide was Jenberu, one who was as trustworthy as the last. His task was to take ten people to the border of Sudan. He, too, carried a gun, a sure sign that this leg of our journey was going to be dangerous. Jenberu knew the area, but it was difficult to get from Negada Baher to Gurva because it was being controlled by rebel groups, so we had to take the road seldom traveled. Because bombs were placed randomly on the ground, set to be detonated by the slightest movement, Jenberu threw stones at various spots and distances. We all ducked, waiting for the explosion.

It was nothing to see limbs and appendages on the roadside, the results of land mines or wild animals. We arrived at Tach Armcheoe, an infamous place to the locals and to the Dergue regime. Because of its geography, mountains and rough terrain familiar only to indigenous peoples, it could not be besieged and taken by force. It seemed as if everyone in Tach Armcheoe was armed, even children. The frequent sound of gunfire was as jarring in the day as it was in the night; I never got used to it.

After Tach Armcheoe, we had to ford Jarma River. If I could get into one of the helicopters, like the one I saw in

Bahar Dar the day I met the *ferenge-och,* and fly over that river, it would look like a winding snake with twelve coils. That's why we had to cross the river twelve times before coming to Tiha after a fifteen-day journey from Negade Baher. At the end of the last coil, Jenburu pointed us in the direction of the border crossing, and then he turned back. We were on our own.

We had gotten this far, so we felt Tiha had to be a good place. We were not prepared for this next obstacle. When we arrived, the soldiers stopped us. We did not know their language, and none of them seemed to understand, or want to understand, Amharic. Although I did not know Arabic, I could understand their gestures; they were separating the men from the women. They moved down the line of refugees, sternly gesturing toward the right in front of the women and toward the left in front of the men. Then they came to us and gestured the same. I did not want them to take Menalu from me. I had some idea of what they would do, for I had heard that men who didn't allow the soldiers to take their wives were killed and that many women had died after being abused sexually by the Sudanese soldiers.

They were waiting for the nighttime when they could take advantage of us, raping us and probably killing us. I knew that something had to be done in the day. Menalu cried. I could hear her weeping and pleading. I tried to convince them that she was my sister, but they seemed totally oblivious to what I was saying. I cried, too, but I really did not even have the strength to cry; I, like Menalu, was hot, tired, hungry, and very frightened.

I, however, found the strength to pray. It was a prayer of desperation, a prayer of ultimatum. "Lord, I have heard a lot about the miracles that you performed for Abraham, Isaac, and Jacob. But we need a miracle. If you are alive, God, where is your miracle? This is the last time I will come to You. I am not willing to give my wife to them. I do not believe you have brought us here to kill us. I do not believe you gave me Menalu only to have her violated or taken from me. Where is your hand? I need to see your hand! I need to see a miracle!"

An hour later, a military jeep came from the city to Tiha, patrolling the border. When I saw the stars on the driver's uniform, I knew he was an officer. So I ran to him, knelt down, grabbed him about the knees, and supplicated him in English: "Please help me." He tried to extricate himself from my grip but he could not; I clung too tightly. "Allah! Allah!" I pleaded. I had heard Arabic people use that as a name for god and I knew they were very afraid of him. This officer spoke English! He could understand me. God was so real!

"We are trying to escape the Dergue regime from Ethiopia," I continued in Amharic. "My parents sent me and my sister together. My mother told me not to lose her, not to separate from her, and they are trying to separate us. Please help us. I would rather die than separate from her." It was then that I understood Abraham's dilemma when he passed off his wife Sarah as his sister.

One of the soldiers knew our culture and history and

had served in the Embassy in Addis Ababa. "*Iyzoh, Iyzoh,*" he said to me in Amharic. It means "Don't worry. Be strong. I will help you."

He spoke to the soldiers, ordered them to leave us alone, and told the women to return to their families. I was reunited with my wife. They allowed us entrance into the border town dotted with small huts—the only protection from the beastly Sudanese sun—occupied by Ethiopian refugees. They gave us food and shelter, and we were incredibly thankful. But I did not want to eat. I could not eat, as I was so full of repentance and gratitude to God that all I wanted to do was thank Him. At the end of my strength and my hope, He was there.

Chapter 16

Khartoum, Sudan—May 1987

THE REFUGEES IN TIHA LET US STAY WITH THEM FOR A WEEK. THEN, some of them found a lorry driver who was taking charcoal from Tiha to Gedariff to Khartoum. An Ethiopian in Tiha assured us that this driver was an honest man. We did not have time to find *tisre* (Arabic word for "passing papers"), which would allow us to move around freely in Sudan. We had to get *tisre* from the security at the border, the place through which we had just miraculously passed, unharmed. We were warned by those in the refugee city not to return to the soldiers to get these papers, a warning we were quite happy to heed.

The lorry driver placed us in the middle of large sacks of charcoal loaded in the back of his truck. At this time,

Menalu wore the Sudanese dress, a long gown with a matching scarf, called a *tov*, wrapped around her head, and I was wearing the white wrap of an Ethiopian peasant. The driver placed a large tarp over the bags of charcoal which concealed our presence as well. There was no flow of air in the back of the truck and at any moment we felt we were going to pass out. The truck came to a complete stop. We knew then we had arrived at the security checkpoint. It was at this time that we had to remain completely still and quiet. There could be no sneezing, no coughing, no movement. If we were caught, we were as good as dead. We heard talking—the very persuasive voice of our driver and then the very commanding voice of another. Eventually, the truck lurched forward. The driver was successful in convincing the border guards that he was not carrying any human cargo, only charcoal. For two hours more we rode in almost unbearable heat, surrounded by sacks of charcoal, in the back of a lorry, which was making its way through a sun-parched Sudan.

Quite a distance from the checkpoint, the driver invited us to sit in the front. Little did I know that he was not inviting *me* to sit in the front; he was only inviting Menalu. She did not want to go alone, so I went with her. At his urging, Menalu sat in the middle. We drove a whole day through the desert and along barren roadway. I was very uneasy because I saw the lustful way he looked at her. After stopping for the night, and continuing the next day, the driver would not leave until Menalu sat in the middle, so during the entire drive he touched her inappropriately. We knew at that point that this Sudanese wanted to take advantage of her. We had no *tisre*, we had no idea where we were going, and we did not speak Arabic, except the few words that Menalu picked up from the time she spent with her father who was a customs officer. As a man, what was I to do? The second night, just before reaching Khartoum, in a small city, he wanted to spend the night; we knew that was the time that he would take her.

Menalu started to heave, back and forth. "I'm sick. I'm sick," she said. "I have to get out." She pretended to vomit.

Angrily, the driver shouted something in Arabic, pulled to a screeching stop, and ordered us out. "Get out!" has a universal understanding, despite the language and culture.

We grabbed our luggage and stood in the middle of that small town, our garments blackened from a two-hour ride with sacks of charcoal, but for us we were standing in the middle of nowhere. When we looked up, out of the darkness running toward us was a mob of ten young men between eighteen to twenty years of age. They shouted, "*Tisre*! *Tisre*!" They wanted to see our papers. "*Betaka*! *Betaka*!" (Arabic for ID card) Passing themselves off as police officers, they could tell that we did not have the items they were requesting. They knew we were foreigners and did not even know their language. This scene had the makings of some of the stories we had heard, of a gang of men taking their turns with helpless women — of men being forced to watch their wives abused and violated. We could not believe that we were about to live through one of those stories! But there we were — nameless characters standing in the darkness, on a sandy street, in some unnamed town—and there was no one around to help us. Who had written this tale for us? I was determined, somehow, some way, to change the ending! They pulled at Menalu's clothes and grabbed her arm. She wriggled, and twisted, and screamed! I tried to fight them off but to no avail.

Ahead of us I saw a light, like a lantern, in front of a building. Who had put it there? What kind of building was it? I did not know that either. All I knew was that we were faced with life and death.

In Amharic, I said to Menalu, "Leave the luggage, and when I give the signal run. Run toward that light." I fought them off her as best as I could, giving her the chance to break free. I gave the signal!

We ran! No where! We ran! Somewhere! We ran toward the light! When we reached the building we burst through the door. It was the home of an *imam,* Arab teacher/priest. He was sitting in a chair, teaching from the *Quran* to young students who sat at his feet. I noticed that the men had pulled off Menalu's *tov,* her headscarf, which cast disrespect upon her and the man whose home she entered.

I kneeled before him, grabbed his hand, and pleaded in English, "Allah, allah, please help me!" It had worked before. I was hoping it would work again.

We could tell he was reluctant to help. We were foreigners. We were dirty. We burst into his home. And

Menalu's head was uncovered.

I pleaded all the more, "Allah, allah, please help me!" Fortunately, this *imam* knew English.

I know some may question what we did, but we give all the credit to the God of Israel who gave us favor with this *imam* who was teaching the *Quran*. In His great wisdom and my ignorance, God worked through this man who was moved to action by the name of his god. Only the God of Israel moves that way and offers no excuses for the way He works.

He got up immediately, went to the door where the mob stood, and angrily said, "Why do you do these things? These people came as guests into our country and you treat them this way. Instead, you should respect them."

Out of deference to the *imam*, the boys left and scattered, disappointed that their maniacal pleasure had been thwarted.

Immediately, this *imam* called his brother who quickly came over. "Please take this couple to your house. Give them food and a place to eat. In the morning, take them to the bus station so that they may go to Khartoum."

Before we left, I went to get our luggage still in the street and then climbed into this man's car. We could tell that he was watching us to see what we would do, how we would act, whether we were related by blood or by marriage. Taking us to his home, he directed us to a bedroom which contained two beds. We quickly moved to separate beds. Then he moved toward Menalu to take her. She had had very little experience praying spontaneous prayers in the name of Yesus, but she prayed. She got on her knees, looked at this man, and then said to him in Arabic, "*Ma thekaf rebek*! Aren't you afraid of Allah? Aren't you afraid of Allah?" This was the Arabic she had learned as the daughter of a customs officer.

Since I still had the money that I brought with us from Tumet, I offered him all the money I had to leave us alone. We had heard that when some Sudanese men see money, and a beautiful woman, it is not unusual that they would take the money, rape the woman, and kill the man. But he took only twenty £, gave me the rest, and left us.

"I *am* afraid of Allah," he said, resignedly. He felt we had been blessed by allah because we had money. Although we were now in the same room, lying in separate beds, Menalu and I still could not fall asleep. We did not know if he was coming back to try again. We knew nothing—only a God of miracles.

In the morning he came, around 5:00, knocking on our door. He took us to the bus station, paid for our tickets, and said, "*Maselama*," an Arabic word meaning "Goodbye."

Our mode of transportation was more of a lorry made into a bus. During the half-day's drive, we had a lot to think about. We had no idea what awaited us in Khartoum, even if we would arrive there safely. We had heard that this was the place they took Ethiopian prisoners. Anytime we saw a police officer, we prayed, "God, help us." We did not speak or look in their direction. Around 1:00 p.m., we arrived in the capital city of Sudan. Everyone got off the bus. What were we to do? In which direction should we walk when we alighted the bus? What language should we speak? We had metal suitcases in our hands, soiled clothes on our bodies—sure indications that we were foreigners. So we started walking—toward the huge capital city of Khartoum.

We saw Ethiopians and tried to talk with them. They did not talk with us or make eye contact. We were invisible to them. Unlike the refugees in Tiha, they were afraid of jeopardizing their own safety.

So we found a place to sit, despondent. Moses had a fire at night and a cloud by day to direct him through the wilderness. We could hardly look at the sky for our sign because of the blinding and oppressive sun. I looked around and met the eyes of an Ethiopian girl was who was looking toward me. "Kokeb?" she asked, walking in my direction. "Are you Kokeb?" she asked incredulously.

"Tsiehay!" I said. She was from Gondar. She ran over and hugged me and I her. It was so good to see a familiar face and to hear a friendly voice. She did not have a house where she could take us, but she knew of a boarding house whose owner rented rooms to Ethiopian refugees with money. After we checked in, we were able to do what we had not done for fifteen days—we took a bath then sat down to eat a hearty meal. During our week-long stay at the boarding house, we felt a great relief from our troubles.

The hub of activity in Sudan was the Sudan Interior Missions Church (SIMC), run by American missionaries.

Various denominations were allowed to use its numerous rooms for their services. This was the place where Ethiopians could get their mail, hang out, fellowship with another, and attend church. Menalu and I started worshipping at Bethel Ethiopian Church for refugees in SIMC every Friday morning, which is the Sudanese Sabbath called *Juma*. We met over 300 Ethiopians; quite a few of them we knew from Gondar.

Some invited us into their homes, even allowing us to stay with them several days. After a week, I knew that I needed to find work, but I did not have *betaka* (an ID card) or *mektebe lamele* (a work permit). The only way to secure one was to find someone who would hire me and apply for my *mektebe lamele*; then I could get *betaka*.

One of our friends found Mansur, a wealthy Sudanese man who owned a music store and an import/export shop in the center of the city of Khartoum. He was looking for a maid, someone to cook and clean for his family. At first Menalu refused because it required that she board in his home Saturday morning through Thursday night after *Juma*. Because of what had occurred in the border town of Tiha, with the lorry driver, and with the Sudanese man, she did not want to be away from me. I told him how my wife felt and asked if I could go with her. He said, "I hired her, not you."

She told him that she would work for him, only if I could come.

"Fine," he said to Menalu and to me he said, "I will find a place for you to stay because you are not allowed to come inside my home." Our new home was the porch of a new building he was erecting, a porch with no roof and no sides. This was Sudan, after all, no rain, no cold temperatures, only dust from the arid soil. We had no running water, no bathrooms, no shelter. So Menalu stayed with Mansur's family during the week and on the porch with me Thursday night to Friday evening, and she brought me the leftovers from their lavish meals.

Even though we had a place to stay and food to eat, I entered another period of depression. My wife was working, and I was not. I worried also about what was going on inside Mansur's house. Sure he had a wife and children, but I had seen too much, images that would never invade the life of an orthodox priest in a Coptic church. The naive twelve-year-old deacon who had only wanted to be with his father and walk into the Holy of Holies was gone. I had gone into Sodom, but did not know whether I had left.

After three weeks, Mansur's wife and children had fallen in love with Menalu. As a result, he offered me a job in one of his stores. With both of us working, we were able to rent a place with fellow Ethiopians, several families living in one room. Menalu asked Mansur to secure work permits for us both. Although he said he would, he did not. He knew that if we had *mektebe lamele* that we would find other jobs; at that moment we were at his mercy. Menalu, especially, worked very hard for his family, night and day, cooking, cleaning, washing, ironing, taking care of their children. Always at their beck-and-call, she hardly ever slept. Her legs were swollen, her hands ached, and she found it difficult to pick up simple items.

Finally she told Mansur, "If you do not give me the *betaka*, I will quit."

He agreed to secure the papers for her. When he received the papers, he gave us a copy and kept the original. He had no concern for us personally. His children loved Menalu, and she had become an indispensable part of his household; he did not want to lose her.

I asked people from Gondar to send me registration papers from Gondar to see if the copy of my *betaka* could be used. The post office alerted me when my papers had arrived. When I went to pick them up, I was told that I needed an ID card to retrieve them. I showed the clerk the photocopy. He laughed at my attempts.

Menalu asked Mansur again, and he complied. After eight months, we held in our hands our *mektebe lamele* and *betaka,* which granted us the privilege to seek better employment. As a result, Menalu gained more freedom on her job. She could go home every day, and eventually, she worked on an "as-needed" basis.

Things were going well, but we knew that such satisfaction would not last. We should have taken a lesson from Jarma River. After crossing one coil of the river, there would be another coil to cross. We should have applied that lesson in every phase of our lives. We overcame the obstacle of our work papers; then Menalu got the news that her father

Melesse was sick, this time for real. To get to him, we had to backtrack. We had to go back to Tiha, then into Tumet. We felt a little more prepared for the journey this time. We could speak a little more Arabic, and the return trip would be easier because we had our *betakas*.

The rebel group controlling Tumet allowed us to go in because they knew her father. When we arrived at Melesse's home, he was already dead, and, according to Jewish custom, buried within twenty-four hours. The family and neighbors were still sitting *shiva,* a period of seven days' formal mourning for the dead, beginning immediately after the funeral.

He had provided shelter for us in Tumet, and he had given us money, without which, we never would have made it to Khartoum. We believed that the God of Israel would honor this old man's dream of living in the Promised Land through his daughter Menalu.

We stayed at my father-in-law's house for one month. Astatek, Menalu's mother, was sick with tuberculosis. We could not leave her in Tumet alone. We traveled with her to Gedariff in Sudan and admitted her into a refugee clinic. We stayed with her for six months, renting a hut, and visiting her every day as she received treatment. If Menalu were going to lose her mother, she wanted to be with her when she took her last breath. She was not there when Melesse passed, so she was determined that this would not be repeated with her mother. After her treatment, we then took her to stay with us in Khartoum for a month. We put her in the care of trusted friends who saw her safely back to Tumet.

Menalu's old job with Mansur had been filled, but Menalu was able to find work with an Italian diplomat. We became very active in the local church. I was an elder in the congregation; I preached on occasion and taught Bible study. Menalu became involved in prayer meetings; she sang in the choir, and she counseled young women dealing with difficult situations. We did not have any sponsors outside of Sudan to support us. Many in our church had support from extended families and Christians all over the world: Australia, America, Canada, and eventually the funding would come so that they could immigrate to these places or receive political asylum. We had no one. We saw airplanes flying above us, and I prayed, "Lord, when is it our time? Will we one day be able to fly out of here?" I had to encourage myself so that I did not get too discouraged and bring sadness to Menalu.

It was at this time that I started hearing about the American dollar, but had never seen one. It was always spoken about with such magic, might, and mystery. It rained down profusely in America, and with it you could do anything.

The coils of the Jarma River wound perpetually in my life. I got the news that my father had passed away. After my mother died, my father had been mother and father to me. Other than Rekebenaha, he was the only family that I knew. Despite my wanting to get as far away from the village of Mo'ta as possible, my desire was never to leave him. When I was in school in Gondar, he came to visit me every other year.

When I worked in the bullet factory in Addis Ababa and the sugar factory in Wonja Showa, I sent him money regularly, so he was always in my thoughts.

My sisters Abren and Assegedech told me later that he felt as if he were the patriarch Jacob and I was Jacob's son Joseph. When Joseph's brothers brought Jacob Joseph's bloodied coat, Jacob thought Joseph was lost to him forever. When my father learned that I had gone to Sudan, it must have been all that his poor heart could take. My leaving the country meant the possibility of my death and emptiness to his dreams of my ever becoming an orthodox priest. When I heard of his death, I wanted to go to the Nile River and just keep walking until I was completely submerged by its waters. I felt guilty and such incredible loss. Many believers came to comfort me. Then God spoke to me in a dream. He showed me that He is my *Abba*. He would not forsake me. He would not leave me. "I am your Father forever," His voice said.

Four years later I found temporary work in the American Embassy as a dishwasher. God gave me favor with the Egyptian manager so that the temporary work became permanent. She promoted me to assistant waiter; ultimately, I became the head waiter. Then she wanted me to learn how to cook by helping the head chef; he, however, did not have the same regard for me as she. He was jealous of the great favor God had given me. My manager sent me elsewhere to learn, and I got a job as a head chef.

With that promotion came another one. I was going to

be a father. Menalu and I had been married for seven years, and in all that time she feared that she was barren. She and a friend had been praying that God would open her womb, and He did. Although Menalu was elated at the news, I did not feel it was a good time to have a child. I did not want to raise a son or daughter in a land where there was no future. Depression came again, this time like snarling hyenas.

My first child, a beautiful daughter, was born in the middle of the day on Good Friday. God had shown us such tremendous mercy through the jungles of Ethiopia and across the border of Sudan that we wanted to commemorate what he had done. We named her Meheret, which means "mercy" in Amharic. She would always remind us of the faithfulness of God's provision.

In the four years of living in Sudan, I had never seen rain. Then God sent, not a shower or a drizzle, but a deluge. The mud houses of the refugees were washed away. All of Sudan suffered, but the refugees suffered the worst. They had no where to live and nothing to eat.

They would stand in long lines for rations of bread, and once they got near the front, the supply would be depleted. Like Joseph who was brought into Egypt so that his people could survive, I, too, saw my purpose. As a cook at the American Embassy, I had access to great supplies. I took all the food that was being thrown away and used it to feed my comrades. Menalu would take the grain that I would bring home and make *kita,* the Sudanese bread. Our house was filled with the hungry, but grateful, people of God.

One day an American political attache, Raymond Southersby (not his real name), came to me while I worked in the kitchen. He said, "I am having a party this weekend with a guest list of about 100 people, and I would like you to cook for me. I will pay you for it." Of course I agreed.

Very impressed with my work, he came back to me after the event and said, "I would like to hire you to work for me full time. I can offer you more money than you are making at the American Embassy. You and your family can stay in an air-conditioned house of an American Diplomat with American furniture. You do not have to worry about your meals." To me that was a miracle! The homes of the refugees in Sudan had no running water, no air conditioning, and no electricity, so Menalu and I saw this as God's provision.

I gave the American Embassy a two-weeks' notice and left. Meheret was almost one when we walked into our two-bedroom home—from refugees to serving an American Diplomat. Our lives were about to turn around in a major way. Then I remembered an event that would eventually enlarge my vision. At the time I was serving as a pastor:

> Before the birth of Meheret, a team of Christian speakers and missionaries (one male pastor and two women) had come from Seattle, Washington to Sudan preach a revival conference. Menalu did not attend because she was pregnant, so I had gone with a friend. The auditorium was divided into three sections: two

side sections and a middle section. I sat in the second row far left facing the front. After the preached word and the altar call, an American woman came forward to say that there would be prayer for healing, and she asked everyone to stand. This woman walked from side to side in front of the audience. Then, of all the people sitting in the meeting, she came directly to me and asked if I could speak English.

I said, "A little." I was too taken aback by her bold approach and the fact that I had been singled out.

"I need a good translator who speaks English well because I have a word from the Lord for you," she said. I told her about a friend I was sitting with who had been a university lecturer in Ethiopia.

Looking directly in my eyes and using her hands for emphasis, she proclaimed, "The Lord speaks to me and says that He will take you out from this country. He will use you mightily. You will go all over the place, to many nations, many, many places."

I had had no experience with prophecy before, so all I could think of was how wrong that woman was. I had no papers, no passport, no money. How could I go from place to place and especially out of the country? I didn't even have a sponsor. This strange woman really does not know what she is speaking about.

The lecturer saw my doubt and disbelief and

told me, "Look, God sent Gabriel to the priest Zechariah to tell him about the blessing that God would give to him, the birth of a son, John the Baptist. And he laughed. God sent the same angel to Miriam to tell her that she would give birth to the Messiah, and she said, '*Hineni.*'[Hebrew for "Here am I"!] This woman, she does not know you, yet out of all the people in this place, she came to you. Why can't you be like Miriam and not like Zechariah? Just say, '*Hineni*'?"

"Okay, okay," I said, "I will believe it." When I got home, I told Menalu the prophecy. I said to her, "God spoke to me in this way, so I must believe. This woman, Idid not know her and she did not know me. So if God provides us any means to leave Sudan, we must go. We must vow together that we will go. We must ask no questions. We only must go. We must do nothing but to serve and trust Him." When she agreed, we prayed together and left it at that.

Letters came from sponsors in America and Australia to resettle the refugees. We applied for assistance but each time we were rejected. We had to present our cases; they wanted to hear stories like the dire events we came out of. That was not our life anymore, so we would not lie on our applications.

Menalu cried and prayed: "God, you gave us this beautiful daughter Meheret. Even if you do not give me a chance to go outside of the country, please send someone who can take care of my daughter, to give her a better life and future. If she goes to school here in Sudan, she will have to learn Arabic and be taught as a Muslim. I do not want that for her. Please send someone who can help."

I thought our help had come through a woman from our church. She worked for a wealthy Egyptian and had asked him if he would secure refugee passports and visas for me and my family. Unfortunately, he could only get me a visa to go to Egypt, but he could not get visas for Menalu and Meheret. Although I was grateful for his kindness, I flatly refused to leave my family in Sudan.

I had worked for Raymond Southersby over eighteen months. We loved him and respected him and believed he felt the same way about us, so we had to tell him the truth. He had always seen me reading my Bible. There was liquor all around me, but I would never drink it. Once he had said to me, "I see that you are a very devoted Christian, a very honest man, Kokeb."

He had always been kind to my family. When he vacationed abroad, he left his car keys with me and brought us gifts from America upon his return. We felt we had to tell him the truth about our Jewishness. Maybe he could help us. We lived in an Arab country, so we knew never to speak of it.

After serving him dinner, I found him sitting in the lobby. Menalu and I knew this was our opportunity to speak to him, so we went together.

"May we speak with you, sir? He took his usual stance, right leg crossed at the knee, left arm over his lap, right elbow resting on the left arm, thumb and forefinger spread apart to rub his mustache and caress his chin. As usual, he was totally unmoved by my request, and in the months I had worked for him, I had never seen him display a range of emotions. Menalu never liked to speak with him alone because of his sternness.

"We need to tell you something. We never wanted to speak of this because we live in an Arab country, and if they knew what we are about to tell you, they would kill us, but we feel we have to tell you. We are Jewish, Ethiopian Jewish. We came as refugees, but we want to go to Israel. Can you help us to get the papers so that we can go?" His face was totally emotionless.

"I am sorry, Kokeb, but it is too late. In three months I will be leaving and going back to Europe. Israel does not have an embassy in Sudan. It's too late, but anyhow I will try."

He tried e-mails but to no avail. After a month, he said, "Forget it, Kokeb. It is impossible." Later on he came to say, "Kokeb, I have good news and bad news. The bad news is that I am leaving very soon. The good news is that even though I am leaving soon, I will turn you over to my replacement, at least you will have a job and a place to stay.'

Again I spent time telling the Lord what He already knew. "Lord, what is happening?" I asked. "*You* promised me these things. This woman, she comes with prophecies about how you will use me, about how I will be traveling from place to place, and I can't even get out of Sudan. It's been almost two years since she told me these things. What is going on?

I've tried this. I've tried that, but nothing."

One day Mr. Southersby came from work. I fed him dinner. When he was finished, I went to him with Meheret in my arms and broached the subject again. "Sir, God has provided you as a messenger for us, an angel; you are the only hope for us," I told him. "Forget about my wife; just take a look at my daughter. I do not want to raise her here in this country. Can you help me to find a way out of Sudan? Can't you take me with you? Are you willing to take me to Europe?"

Still unmoved he said, "I can't take you to Europe. There are three of you. Even if I tried to get you into Egypt, your family could not get passports. Even if I wanted to take *you, you* don't have a passport." I knew that if we did not get out soon, the three of us would turn into four. Menalu was pregnant with our second child.

"It is true, I do not have a passport, but you are an American. If you write me a letter to the United Nations High Commissioner for Refugees (UNHCR), they will give me a travel document."

"Do you really think that, Kokeb?"

"Yes, sir, I do."

The next day he wrote a letter for us, and I went to the office of the UNHCR to get the travel document. Needless to say, they turned down my request. I was angry when I left and even angrier when I relayed the story to Mr. Southersby.

He told me that he had a person working in the Embassy who would help us, a Sudanese man. "He will go with you," he said. He contacted this man who went with me and within minutes, we had our passports.

The next day he took our passports to the Egyptian Embassy to secure our visas. An official at the Embassy said, "Sir, we cannot give Egyptian visas to Ethiopians with refugee passports. If we do, when these people get into Egypt, they will try to apply for government assistance. We cannot give government help to refugees. We have been instructed not to give visas to refugees."

I did not know how much I could take of the highs and lows of hope and disappointment. It was like riding the craggy slopes of the Blue Nile Gorge. But I would not give up. The shut-eyes-squeezed-tightly approach would not work this time, so I went back to him.

"I know, Kokeb, that you are persistent, but I have tried my best. The Egyptian Embassy will not give you an Egyptian Visa for a refugee document."

"Sir," I relentlessly told him, "our lives are in your hands. If you leave us, we have no other chance. You are our only hope. I believe there is another way. If you write a letter to the Ethiopian Embassy saying that you are taking us with you as workers—because you are an American, they might give us an Ethiopian Passport."

With his chin resting between thumb and index finger, he said, with an even-temper, "And you think this will work, Kokeb?"

Yes, sir," I do.

"Okay, I will try," he said. He wrote the letter.

The next day I went to the Ethiopian Embassy and presented them the letter. They were furious. "You mean you hate our country this much that you would go to Sudan as a refugee and then expect to get a passport in one day. Get out of here!" This thrust me into a state of deep, overwhelming discouragement.

I walked away from the Ethiopian Embassy for the long walk back home. I had tried everything I knew to do, so I prayed. "God," I cried to this long-suffering Deity who had heard from me as if I were His only child and petitioner, "You spoke to me through this woman. I did not know her. She did not know me. She called me out of 300 people and told me something so farfetched that even at that time I did not believe it. But I have chosen to believe it. I have chosen to believe that You will take me out of Sudan. That You will use me for your glory. I need to see Your hand, God! I feel as if I have done all I can do. I need to see Your hand." In the book of Isaiah (41:21), God told his people, "Produce your cause; bring forth your strong reasons." I was doing just that to a God who had said that he wanted to work miracles that were far beyond my thoughts and my imagination.

I knew that I could not go back home with such hopeless news. Mr. Southersby needed to know what had happened. I did not know what else he could do, but he needed to know that I was not successful, so I made the forty-five-minute walk in the oppressive Sudanese heat from the

Ethiopian Embassy to the American Embassy. When I told Mr. Southersby what had happened, he told me to sit, motioning to the chair across from his desk. Then he picked up the phone and called the Ethiopian Ambassador in Khartoum, Sudan.

"Look, I am trying to help your citizens, your people," Mr. Southersby said sternly. I sat and listened to him. I had never heard him speak so menacingly before. "I am trying to take them to Egypt to help them, but you refuse to give them a passport? Why? What is the reason? If you do not give them a passport, I will write an article about your Embassy and send it all over the world so that people will know what you are doing to your own people."

The man on the phone denied ever seeing me and passed it off as someone else's negligence. They encouraged Mr. Southersby to send me back to the Embassy.

"Give me another American to go with me, and I will go," I told him. This was such a crucial point in my life and time did not seem to be on my side. Also, they had dismissed me so emphatically that going alone, I believed, would cause them to disdain my goal even more.

He summoned one of his young American workers and a diplomat car to take us to the Embassy. I was too busy praying that the encounter would be successful that I did not realize I was being treated like Biblical Mordecai, Queen Esther's uncle. He had been given the king's horse; I was now riding in a diplomat's car.

When we arrived at the Ethiopian Embassy, the workers

were very accommodating, almost falling over themselves wanting to assist the American.

The Ambassador from the Ethiopian Embassy spoke with me and asked me what had happened. I told him the story. They called for someone working in the visa section of the Embassy. After the Ambassador spoke with the American Embassy representative, the Ambassador asked me if I had the passport pictures. I had been waiting for this very moment, so I had everything that we needed: a photo of me and one of Menalu and Meheret together. I gave the pictures to them immediately. Within moments, seemingly, they were placing in my hands our passports. What normally takes a person years to receive, we possessed after many tears, much determination, great favor, and another miracle.

Then, the next day Mr. Southersby went to the Egyptian Embassy with our Ethiopian passports. He was told that he had to write a letter saying that he took full responsibility for me and my family as we traveled with him to Egypt. Five days later, Mr. Southersby told us that he had all the documentation we had requested, so we needed to be ready to go with him in one week.

We had served Bethel Ethiopian Church for almost six years. I was one of the main leaders of the congregation. Usually when someone in the congregation got foreign support to immigrate, the church would throw a party. We had nothing to show—not passports, not plane tickets, nothing. Mr. Southersby had not given us the visas. He kept them, saying that he was trying to protect us. All we had to do was prepare to leave. It was hard to believe we would be leaving when we had no paperwork. It was even harder to tell the congregation that we were leaving when we had nothing to show them.

"Sunday I will be leaving Sudan with my family," I told them, trying to prepare them for the inevitable.

"Where are your visas?" someone asked. "Show us the documents!" someone else shouted.

"We do not have them." People chuckled.

They did not take us seriously. They just assumed it was wishful thinking on our part. I preached during the Friday and Sunday morning services. Sunday at 6:00 p.m., Mr. Southersby called and asked me if we were ready. We gathered our luggage. When the diplomat's car pulled up in front of our home, we got in and he drove us as a final farewell through the very familiar city of Khartoum to the international airport. Mr. Southersby had not asked us to pay for our tickets, although I assured him that I would pay for them, but he had already bought them.

"We are about to go through security," he said. "I just need you to follow me." If anyone other than an American diplomat possessed an American dollar, that person would be arrested; that's what I discovered later. I had an American dollar in my pocket.

"I am an American Diplomat," Mr. Southersby told the man at customs. We followed Mr. Southersby rigidly; if he walked to the right, we walked to the right. If he veered left; we veered left. When he walked straight through customs, we walked behind him, right through customs, I with an American dollar in my pocket, but walking with an American Diplomat.

As we boarded the plane, we were both gripped with separation anxiety leaving the place that had been our home for six years. We had made many friends and built many spiritual altars in the places we had lived and visited. I had looked at airplanes flying in the sky wondering when it would be our turn. I had said that we had no extended families, no benefactors from other countries to assist us. But we were living in the home of a man who would be our Moses. Imagine looking to a plane in the sky for help when help is right before you. Imagine, looking across the water for aid when you are serving water to your Moses.

We traveled by night on Luftanza Airlines, not as refugees, but as ambassadors. We were determined to be one country closer to the Promised Land.

Chapter 17

Cairo, Egypt—1993

WE ARRIVED IN CAIRO IN THE MORNING, 1993. WE HAD TO GO through customs again. Mr. Southersby passed easily. The agent looked at our Ethiopian passports then looked at us.

"Wait here," he told us. He was about to call someone to interrogate us, possibly to put us in jail or send us back to Sudan. After waiting thirty minutes, I concluded that maybe they needed money from us. Maybe I should give them money.

"Where are our passports?" I asked.

At that time, Mr. Southersby came back to us. "Why aren't you letting them through?" Mr. Southersby asked the agent.

"Who? Them?" he asked incredulously.

"Yes, them," Mr. Southersby said. "Kokeb and Menalu Gedamu." Is this the way God will call our names forth on that great day when we pass from this world into the next—with such authority that no one will be able to question Him?

"Oh, they are with you," he said ingratiatingly. "So sorry, sir, so sorry."

They let us through. Another diplomat car arrived to pick us up. I told them to take us to a church in Zemalik, for someone was waiting for us there. When we arrived, he waited for us, making sure that we were connected with friends. He gave me his telephone number and told me to call him the next day. From the church, one of the congregants took us to his house.

I called Mr. Southersby the next day and he told me to go to the American Embassy in Cairo. When I arrived, he introduced me to an American Diplomat and had me apply for a work permit that had to be renewed yearly. "If you have any financial problem," he said, "let me know." Then he gave me $500 just in case I had any difficulty getting my family settled. In three days he left Cairo. His friend applied for a work permit for us the following week; then the following week they took me to the Israeli Embassy. I asked others where the Israeli Embassy was located. When I said the word "Israel," I was hushed and warned. It was taboo to say that word in Egypt. We were told to say, "A small country." The Egyptians had heard about Ethiopian Jewry, so they were very skeptical and cautious of Ethiopians. I went to the American Embassy and was introduced to the Israeli consulate. I told him our history and that my wife and I were Jewish and wanted to go to Israel. "We have been working so that we can go to Israel. We have been in Sudan for six years," I told him.

"Do you have evidence that you are Jewish?"

We looked at each other. "Our parents are Jewish."

"But do you have any evidence, any proof?" he asked nonchalantly, revealing his frequent dealings with refugees with a similar plight

We had none.

"So," he said, "you have no evidence that you are Jewish? Furthermore, no Jew can make *aliyah* [immigration] to Israel from an Arab country; you were not born in Egypt but in Ethiopia. The government of Ethiopia has changed."

It had been three years since we crossed the border from Metema into Tiha, Sudan. The Dergue government was overthrown in '91. He was right—life in Ethiopia had changed. "You may return if you like," he said. "There will be no harm to you and your family."

There was no need for us to return to the Embassy. There was nothing that he could do for us. We had to find work so that we could survive. Menalu, in her ninth month of pregnancy, found work as a housekeeper, and I found a job as a cook. We needed to connect spiritually to a community since Egypt was going to be our home until God performed another miracle. We found a group of Ethiopians who gathered just to fellowship, so I sensed the leading of the Lord to establish a church, a big church; we called it Maranatha Evangelical Ethiopian Refugee Church. It still exists today, thriving in

Cairo, Egypt. Our congregation consisted mostly of refugees with no income. Fortunately, a missions organization allowed us to meet for free in their building. We had to pay the rent for our home ($100 monthly) and still survive. We were financially strapped. Then, Mr. Southersby's friend left, the one he had commissioned to take care of us.

On top of the current crisis, our second child was born. When God gave Israel victory over the Philistines in I Samuel 7, the prophet Samuel took a stone and placed it between Mizpah and Shen, the place where the battle had been won. Samuel named the stone "Ebenezer" because "Thus far," he says, "the Lord has helped us." Up to this point in our lives, God had been our help. Despite our present difficult situation, we wanted to commemorate what God had done, so we named our son Ebenezer.

After one year our work permits would expire and no one would renew them because they were only issued to official workers for diplomats. We had not expected to stay so long. When we came to Cairo, we thought the Embassy would accept us and send us to Israel. Sometimes I did not have fifteen cents to catch the bus to teach the weekly Bible study. In those times, I walked two hours just to get to the service. Things were not changing. There was no food at home. We were using candles in place of electricity. Meheret was three with greater demands for food. The only one who was being fed was our baby Ebenezer. All of this was happening, and I served the Lord. I did not understand. We cried. We cried too much. There was no money. There was no food to eat. We cried. The children cried. "Mom, I am hungry," Meheret whined daily.

I was a cook. I had to find work to feed my family. Fortunately, I had gathered letters of recommendation from the American Embassy in Khartoum and from Mr. Southersby, so I had the references I needed. Someone told me that a famous Egyptian singer was looking for a cook who could prepare American food. Impressed with my references, she hired me. After working for almost one week, she invited to dinner a friend of hers whom she had told of my exceptional culinary skills. I wanted to please her and impress her guest. I could hear them in amiable chatter as I approached the dining room, carrying the platter, beautifully prepared and garnished. Just before reaching the table where they sat, my legs gave way and I fell flat on my backside, and sent the platter flying in one direction and the food in another. She was so disappointed that she cried as her friend tried to console her. She called a taxi, gave me my wages, and told me not to return.

I did not know what was happening. Normally, I was a healthy person. I had never been sick. And I did not remember slipping, getting dizzy, or losing my balance when I was serving them. When I returned home, everything was normal. I felt fine. Although I was disappointed that I had lost my job, I now had a little money, and I could feed my family.

A week later I heard that an English Diplomat was looking for a cook. I worked with him during the week, preparing his meals. I received nothing but praises for the quality of the food. Within a week, he told me his whole family, children and grandchildren, were coming to visit. That Saturday night, he said he would show me how to prepare English food. Saturday came and I was excited about expanding my culinary knowledge and ability. He asked me to take out all the ingredients for plum pudding. He told me what to mix and how high the oven should be set. As he showed me how to prepare the meal, sweat was forming suddenly on my brow. My stomach felt queasy. I started to heave, and before I knew it, I had thrown up in his beautiful kitchen in the midst of making a meal that he knew his family would enjoy. He called the maid to clean up the kitchen. "Thank you, Kokeb," he said. "Here is some money. Please do not come back. Just go." When I got home and told Menalu what had occurred, she was puzzled because there was no indication that I was sick. I was fine. I had not felt sick before the incident, and I did not feel sick at that moment.

We had a close friend whom we considered family, a member of our congregation; her name is Hannah, a woman of prayer. Today she lives in Australia. When I arrived at my apartment, she was there. I had told her about the prophecy from the American missionary who had come to Sudan. When I told her about the incident in the European Diplomat's home, she asked, "Didn't you promise the Lord that you would serve Him? Didn't you promise Him that you would do His work? Why are you looking for a job now? Maybe that's why these things are happening. Maybe you're getting off course."

"What do you mean, 'off course'?" Menalu asked. "We have nothing to eat. I have two small children. They need food."

"If you promised Him you would work for Him," she said doggedly in her seemingly harsh response, "you must do it at all cost. God will provide what you need."

She knew that telling someone to be faithful in a difficult situation was no easy task, so she tried to help us remain faithful by sharing with us what little she had. She did not have much money, so her assistance could not support herself and my family. Then Menalu and I started to pray, our words, swaddled in tears, going up to God. "Look at our children! They do not have anything to eat. But I serve you. I want to work, but you are not allowing me to work. But I still serve you. My Ebenezer cries every night, all night. He can't sleep. *We* can't sleep. But we serve You!"

At about 5:30 a.m., someone called me; it was Seble, one of the choir members in my church. Usually when one got a call that early, it was to report a death. Menalu started crying thinking that the news was about her mother. The children started crying all over again when they saw her weeping.

"Sabba and I are coming over," Seble said. Before we go to work, we must stop by." I knew it. Someone *must* have died. They could not tell us on the phone. They just had to come over in person to tell us. With such nervous anxiety, we waited in our second floor apartment for their arrival. When we heard the car drive up, we went to the window. Seble and

Sabba were getting out of a taxi and unloading a number of packages, which appeared to be grocery bags. They knew that we would need food. When someone died, it was customary to bring food to serve the guests.

"Tell us who has died," I demanded, more concerned about the news than the food.

"Sit down first," Seble commanded. "No one has died. God spoke to us last night and told us to do this. I have saved $300 to send to my mother in Ethiopia. God told me to go to the store and buy everything that you need with the $300 I had saved." I do not know if I could have loved God any more than I did at that moment. In the past He had saved *my* life and *Menalu's* life many times, but now He had added my children to that list.

Sabba and Seble had bought everything that we needed: oil, diapers, sugar—everything. They said that God told them to pick this, pick that. Who said that God does not know what we need? Who said that God is not concerned about us? You may call it a coincidence; I call it a miracle!

Sabba said, "I have $200 that I have been saving 'just in case.' God told me to give it to you. Here is $200 for you."

After we prayed for them, they left and went to work. God had brought them into our lives, woke them up in the middle of the night, put our names into their minds, and our needs upon their hearts. He chose two faithful ones who would not *just* pray but would *act* and act so unselfishly. They gave of their time. They gave of their resources. They gave their savings. Father, bless Seble (who lives in America now) and Sabba (a pastor in Egypt) immeasurably.

Menalu and I asked the Lord's forgiveness. Our lives had been forever changed because God had done what I had not even imagined.

God was really moving among the members of my church. They were being filled with the Spirit and being obedient to the Lord in their giving. They were able to take care of my rent. After eleven months in Cairo, I wanted to sponsor a conference. I invited a singer from Ethiopia to come to Cairo as a guest in our church. He stayed in our home for eleven months. One day the phone rang; the caller was an Ethiopian doctor who lived in Germany. Dr. Henok wanted to meet the singer to invite him to Germany for a conference. He planned to go to Israel first, then to Cairo to meet with the singer. We gave him our address, and he promised to come the following week.

In Egypt, we were so close to Israel but were never able to find that bridge that would take us across. Therefore, we had settled down in Egypt like the Israelites in Goshen, the land of their provision, but now God would send a bridge through Dr. Henok and awaken us to the original intent of our journey.

Chapter 18

Israel—July 1994

A WEEK LATER, DR. HENOK ARRIVED AT OUR HOUSE AND GREETED Menalu, me, and our two children. He told us of his travels to Israel, of seeing the Holy Land and all the places that Yesus Kristos had walked. He told of the sacred feeling that overwhelmed him when he visited Jerusalem and stood at the Wailing Wall. As he recounted all that he had seen, Menalu started to cry. "Honey, why are you crying?" I asked.

"What is wrong?" Dr. Henok asked, feeling guilty about what he had said or done, but not knowing exactly what it was that prompted her tears.

Finally, now able to speak, Menalu said to him, "I am Jewish, but I do not have any means to go to Israel because I cannot find my family."

"You are Jewish?!" the singer asked, surprised.

Menalu became a little frightened, realizing what she

had said and what he could possibly do with the information.

I was surprised, too. This was a secret that Menalu had kept from others throughout her life, and now she had met a stranger and not only did she begin to cry, but also she had revealed a long-kept secret. At that point, I, too, had to reveal my ancestry.

He laughed and cried. He hugged her! He kissed her. "How blessed I am to come to the home of one of the blessed families!" he said. His joy was almost uncontainable. "I love the Jewish people!"

Never in our lives had anyone received the identity of our Jewishness in such a way. In the past it was something that was kept quiet, hush-hush. Even the use of the name "Israel" in Egypt was forbidden. Now, my wife and I were being blessed and lauded because we are Jewish. I could never have invented such an ironic twist to our story. But the God of Israel, the God of paradoxes and absurdities—He could!

She told him her whole story. He reiterated his devotion to the Jewish people and shared about the work that he was doing in Israel to acclimatize Ethiopian Jews to their new home. He left and when he returned later that night, he hugged us and kissed us again. Then he asked us for our family names. We gave him photographs of us, and he told us that he would return in three days and promised us that if we had family in Israel, he would help us find them. Then he found Breley, a believer in Israel, and gave him our names, pictures, and letters to our family.

Israel hosted a government-sponsored Amharic-speaking radio station that ran for one hour in the middle of the day. Every Ethiopian Jew in Israel listened to that station because they did not speak Hebrew or Arabic fluently, or because it reminded them of home. The station made frequent announcements about Ethiopian Jews searching for relatives in Israel. One fateful day, an announcement was made about us:

"Kokeb Gedamu and Menalu Melesse are looking for their families. If you are relatives of Menalu Melesse or Kokeb Gedamu, please contact the radio station as soon as possible. Tirue Melesse or Aynaw, if you are in Israel, please contact the radio station."

Tirue and Asynew, Menalu's sister and her husband, told us later that when they heard our names, they cried because they thought that we had died. They called the station, which put them in contact with Dr. Henok. He met them, gave them our pictures and phone number, and they contacted us in Cairo immediately. For almost one hour Menalu talked and cried with her sister and family. An Ethiopian Jew with the Interior Ministry called us two days later and interviewed us by phone. Want to hear another miracle? The interviewer Enyew was from Gondar so we knew him and his family. I knew of another Israelite who had to endure great hardships to be united with his family. Only our families had not betrayed us the way Joseph's brothers had, and our reunion was much sweeter.

The interviewer told us to get prepared to leave Egypt.

He told us that someone would contact us; then we would be in Israel soon. That day, Mr. Roni called us to come to the Israeli Embassy. He was the same one who refused us a year ago, telling us not to return. Now he was calling me, telling me to come with our passports but not to bring my family. I left as quickly as I could.

"We know that you are Jewish now because we have received the evidence," he told me. "Leave your passport here. Be ready to make aliyah Sunday." Today was Thursday.

"How can I leave Sunday with such short notice?" I asked. I was the pastor of a thriving congregation. I could not just disappear, but I knew that it would not be wise to mention the church, so I said, "I have an important document coming from Ethiopia. I need to wait one more week." It was true that I was expecting papers from home, but they were not important enough for me to delay my trip…but my congregation was.

He asked for our passports and told us not to worry about the tickets. In one week, he said, we would be flying to Israel; that would give me enough time to set some things in order. I got up Sunday morning as usual—but it would not be a usual Sunday—and prepared for my last Sunday, my last day in Cairo. Since our congregation was given space in a church, we held our services in the afternoon.

At the end of my sermon, I said, "Today, I am going somewhere with my family. I do not yet know where I am going, but I will be leaving. When I leave, this man," I said, putting my hand on the shoulder of the one next to me, "will be your leader. I will come back but I do not know when." We ordained the elder from the ministry staff as a pastor. "Where are you going?" they asked. This was the second time we had found ourselves in this situation—of secrets about where we were going and the uncertainty of whether we would go.

"We want to be able to throw you a party. Tell us where you are going," someone shouted

"I cannot say," I said. After I preached the sermon, Menalu and I returned home. We gathered our luggage and two children and took a taxi to the Cairo airport without tickets or passports. When we drove up, two well-dressed Israeli men met us. "Are you Kokeb Gedamu?" one of them asked.

"Yes," I said.

"Are you Menalu Gedamu?"

"Yes," she said.

"Are these your children?"

We both answered, "Yes."

"Grab your things and come with us," one of them said. Sensing our anxiety, he continued, "We are Jewish, too, so do not be afraid. You will be fine." They showed us our tickets and passports and said we would be flying on El Al. They took us to a special location, making sure that our luggage was secure, and tried to make us comfortable by giving us towels, blankets, and food. The plane was due to arrive at midnight. On July 19, 1994, we boarded the El Air Airlines and flew into Tel Aviv, Israel. Melesse, Menalu's father, believed that Menalu would be the seed that entered the Promised Land. Yet as he slept in Ethiopian soil, his three daughters would inherit his promises and walk the land of his fathers.

My father had told me that I was a child of *Wolte Yisrael,* (Mother Israel). He said that I was a Levite, one of the *kohanim*. Everywhere I had gone, from Ethiopia to Egypt, I lived the Word of God; now I would have the opportunity to live it in the land of my forefathers, on Jewish soil. I was going home to my mother, *Wolte Yisrael.* I was going to live my father's silent dream and discover thoughts that he could never share. I could hardly believe that this moment had come. Little did I know that the six years I would spend in Israel would challenge me more than all the previous years.

When we arrived in Tel Aviv in the middle of the night, Zevina, a worker with the Interior Ministry met us, speaking in Amharic. He gave us picture ID cards and called a taxi to pick us up to take us on a two-hour journey to Haifa. He told us, "Your driver does not know how to speak Amharic, but trust him. He will take you to the place where you will be living." He dropped us in *caravanim,* a temporary holding place for newcomers. Unfortunately, the office opened at 8:00 a.m., so we had to wait. Eventually, a woman came, saw that we looked tired, and let us in to rest. We did not care how long it would take or how uncomfortable we were–we were in the Promised Land. We could hardly contain out tears of joy. We longed to be reunited with our family. Finally, at 8:00 officers came, checked us in, and took us to our new home.

"This is your new home," one of them said, showing us a one-bedroom mobile home. "This is your house, your furniture, your washer." For one year, the government will provide a monthly income. You will be given the opportunity to learn the Hebrew language. Your children will go to school. Remember, this is temporary housing, until you are able to provide for yourselves." They brought us an extra cot for Meheret and a crib for Ebenezer. We were reborn! Our long awaited home, our country, had just reached out and cradled us. All the struggles! All the hardships! The trying of our faith! The tears! It was all worth it! It was all worth it!

Right away we entered a one-year program for newcomers to learn Hebrew, *ulpan,* for beginners. The local Israeli rabbi came to us asking us to make *giur*. He wanted us to make a public statement of our embrace of Judaism by being immersed again and by my being re-circumcised. In so doing, we were making a declaration of our uncleanness and our willingness to be made clean by the procedure. We learned later that many Ethiopians were going through this ritual, but I refused. "If you do not do it," the rabbi said, "your ID cards will say, 'Christian' or 'Ethiopian,' not 'Jewish,' so your children will have no rights. They cannot be married or buried in Jewish ceremonies."

Some Ethiopians encouraged us to make *giur*. "You don't understand," they said. "If you don't do this, you will make it very difficult for your children." Part of making *giur* was attending prayer with the rabbis and going to the Beit

Kinesset for doctrinal studies and workshops. I refused to do anything that was intended for me to renounce my faith.

I did attend the Hebrew workshops which were like a social club. I met many friends from Gondar and from Sudan, one of them, Meseret, who knew of my faith, told me about an underground Messianic congregation in Natanya, which met every two weeks. Two weeks later I went with her and found the believers. Other Ethiopians had warned me not to go, that it would interfere with the immigration process. Because of the believers' fear of the government and the Orthodox Ethiopians, they did not allow just anyone to come into the congregation, so I had to be invited. I left Menalu with the children and went to check out the meeting. Forty or fifty members came from all over Natanya, met in a home where they also lodged for the weekend, praying, studying the Word of God, and fellow-shipping.

Two months later, Menalu and I were attending the congregation together. Initially, she was very frightened but became more comfortable as we continued. A year later in 1995, we found a new home and moved our family from Haifa to Rehoboth. I noticed that the Ethiopian Messianic believers were divided into four groups—Jerusalem, Nazareth, Natanya, Tel Aviv—and that the intense friction among them kept them separated. It would be difficult enough to grow the congregation while underground, but with infighting, it would be almost impossible. So, I started a phone campaign to bring unity among the congregations. I asked for a ride or took a bus to meet them personally. I asked each leader's permission to organize a reconciliation prayer meeting where all of them could come together and pray for the same purpose with the same focus. I arranged a meeting at an English mission guest called Beth Emmanuel in Jaffa, Tel Aviv, where we could eat together and fellowship for two days and one night. I ministered to them, and then I asked them to forgive each other, and they did. Animosity had existed among these leaders for five or six years, but God moved upon their hearts and gave each one the spirit of forgiveness. They tasked me with the responsibility to call them again.

A friend in Ashkelon helped me organize another meeting, this time not specifically for prayer, but a strategic meeting to merge our efforts. Three of the four groups were willing to participate. We were able to sit down together, form a constitution, and agree to select new leadership for the merged congregation. After the new constitution was approved by the leaders, almost a year later, we held a meeting for all the members from the different congregations. We shared with them the constitution, and all resolved to choose leadership for the new group.

The people chose me as their leader. The younger leader refused to work with us. I pleaded with him to stay and told him that I would work under him. He said no and resigned. So I was the leader, the chairman of the underground Ethiopian congregation that we named Torch of Gideon, about sixty members strong. We had no money, so I encouraged the elders to apply for *amutta,* nonprofit status. They reasoned that applying for nonprofit status meant becoming more public. They preferred to operate secretively because they feared that they would be deported and their families who remained in Ethiopia would not be allowed to make *aliyah.* Tension between me and the leadership grew, but I moved forward anyway. I chose seven young members who were willing to go to the Interior Ministry, who were not afraid to show their ID cards and start the application for *amutta* for our congregation. We owed a great deal of gratitude to an Israeli lawyer who helped us to establish the nonprofit organization. Because of his efforts, it only took one month for us to receive government-recognized *amutta.*

As stated in our *amutta,* one of our purposes was to preach boldly, not only from *Torah* and *Tenach,* but also from the *Brit Hadashah,* the *New Testament.* We also included that we would meet monthly with Messianic leaders to pray and encourage one another in the faith. We were the only Messianic believers to make such bold claims on our application. The others wrote only about their religious studies.

Months later, I received an invitation from a church in Finland to share about the plight of Ethiopian Jewry. They had received my name from a missionary from Finland who worked closely with Ethiopian Messianic communities, long before I arrived in Israel. I knew that my English was not adequate to convey the story of my people; therefore, I said no. "Don't worry," they wrote, "we have an Ethiopian missionary in our congregation who speaks Amharic. Just come. She will translate for you." I applied for a passport, but even after receiving my plane ticket, the reality of the event had still not settled.

Before the plane landed in Finland, I looked out the window to see a heavy, white cloud. Maybe it appeared thick, three-dimensional, and almost tangible because I was so close to it, but it was in a form unlike one I had ever seen. In my heart I said, "Holy Spirit, come to me." As we went through it, I felt as if I were being immersed into the Holy Spirit for the first time. I heard a voice speaking Amharic. It was so audible that I had to turn around to see who was speaking, but no one was looking at me, and I was the only Ethiopian on the plane. "Kokeb," the gentle voice said, "remember the woman who prophesied to you in Sudan? I spoke through her and she told you that I would use you. That you will go all over the world. That prophecy is starting today. This is the beginning of the rest of your journey." Tears trickled because I had forgotten about the prophecy, and God spoke to me, reminding me of His promises.

After that event, I received invitation after invitation. One of them was to Germany, where I stayed for two weeks. As I traveled, I told churches of my vision to build a congregation in Israel, and people began to sow seed into that vision. I was able to raise a half million shekels. The Lord blessed the ministry financially and spiritually. When God worked in the realm that was beyond our imagination, we knew that opposition would increase. When God gave Joseph visions and dreams and favor with his father Jacob, Joseph's brothers became jealous and despised him. So did it happen with me. When the money was sent to the congregation, I was even accused of extorting some of it.

But where sin abounds grace abounds even more. God began to open heavenly windows that I had not even envisioned, and rained down blessings from unexpected sources, like the story of Esther born in Ethiopia to Swiss missionary parents. Because she was born and raised in Ethiopia, she could speak a little Amharic. This is the story she relayed to me when we spoke:

> When her parents returned to Switzerland, she returned with them but always had a heart for Ethiopians. She had a friend, an older woman who had heard about Operation Moses and Operation Solomon, the daring rescues of Ethiopian Jews from Sudan into Israel. Before she passed, she had given Esther money to send to Ethiopian believers in Israel.
>
> "I don't know anyone in Israel, so how can I send the money to them?" Esther had asked her.
>
> "Put it in the bank," she said.
>
> "How can I? It's not my money!"
>
> "Put it in the bank. God will tell you when and where to send it."
>
> She did just as the woman had told her and prayed. That was in 1991. In 1995 Esther heard that a

Messianic leader from Israel was coming to Switzerland to preach. When she found out the particulars, she drove seven hours to hear him. Making a point of meeting him after he spoke, she told him she had been given money to donate to Ethiopian believers in Israel and asked if he could give it to them.

"How much is it?" he asked.

"Around 40,000 *euros,*"she said.

"How can I take that much money?" he asked. "This is what you can do," he continued. "Give me your contact information, and I will forward it to the leader of their congregation. Then, he can contact you."

At the next monthly prayer meeting for Messianic leaders, he gave me her information and I contacted her. Communicating mostly in Amharic, I gave her the bank name and she deposited the money. We started with nothing. Now our organization had over 100,000 *shekels*. We asked the Lord how could we use it to increase His Kingdom?

After meeting with the Messianic believers in Israel and learning more Hebrew, I became acquainted with the Hebrew Name of *Yesus, Yeshua,* and *Kristos, Hamaschiach,* Christ, the Anointed One. I knew from that point on I wanted to use His Hebrew name when I spoke to Him or about Him. Also while in Israel, we changed Meheret's name to Ruhama, her Hebrew name which also means "mercy."

In 1996, God increased my family as he had increased

our finances. My third child, a daughter, was born in the Promised Land, a *sabra*. It was more than we could ask. She was beautiful, healthy and delivered under much better care in Rehoboth Hospital, my father's seed, Melesse's seed sprouting forth in Israel. We named her Tsiona (See o´ na), because she greeted this world in Zion.

With the increase in our finances and family, I also prayed about how to expand the congregation. We organized a large conference in a Messianic Jewish *moshav,* a housing development. This was the first time Ethiopian believers had gathered from the four-city area to attend a weekend conference. I invited a well-known speaker from America to preach, an Ethiopian pastor, Seifu Kebde, whose passion was revival. He and his wife Evangelist Tsigewongel became my spiritual parents and Pastor Seifu eventually ordained me as a pastor, an office, he felt, I had been fulfilling all along. Although not Jewish himself, he has a great love for Ethiopian Jewry and a desire to see us operate in our spiritual authority.

At the revival conference, under his ministry, people were being healed from diseases and set free from demonic activity, ultimately liberated to receive all that God had for them. We recorded the services with the purpose of duplicating videos so that people could purchase them and view them in their homes, reminding them of all that God had done. In six months, our membership grew from sixty to 150. In five years 400 believers in Yeshua came seeking more of God at our congregation.

As it is in the natural, so it is in the spiritual. A number of problems developed. The Orthodox Ethiopian Jews spoke out against us, claiming that we were not Jewish. The government spoke against me, specifically. The older leaders did not want the visibility that my leadership was bringing to the congregation; they wanted the movement to remain underground. They also did not want to release the video, for they believed that we would incur too many problems if the government got its hands on it. This had been a move of God, and no one had a right to squelch what the Holy Spirit was doing. So without their permission, I allowed the media ministry to duplicate the video to be used in people's homes.

Some who bought a copy took to it to the Interior Ministry. This caused major problems for my family and the Israeli government. They put clips of the video on national television. They said, "Look at what the Ethiopians are doing, claiming to be Jewish when they are not! They are bringing a curse upon us! They have brought demonic activity to our country!" My name was plastered across the screen in big letters: "The leader of this group is Kokeb Gedamu." Radio stations started carrying the same broadcast. Politicians and mostly members of the Orthodox Ethiopian Jewish community called my house, frightening my wife.

"He is going to die," they told her. "We have been keeping our Jewish religion for 3000 years. Now when he comes to Israel, he is changing our children into Christians. He must be stopped, and if we have to go to jail for stopping him, that is what we prefer. We do not care about dying if he dies."

My mind was caught in a vise grip. Inside, the older leaders in the congregation were against me. Outside, government persecution of me and my family haunted me. But I remained focused on what the Lord was doing in the lives of those who had been freed because of the ministry. That brought me some consolation.

Then, I brought my brother Libanos from Ethiopia to Israel as a visitor. As a child, my father only shared with me that I was a Levite; he never told me of my Jewish heritage. When I married Menalu, I was able to come to Israel because of her Jewish identity, but I had grown very interested in discovering my Jewish roots. My older siblings knew the story, but had never shared it with me. My brother had searched our roots, found our relatives in Israel, and he had applied at the Interior Ministry to become a citizen. They told him, "Your brother is a missionary. He is preaching Christianity and changing many young people from Judaism to Christianity. Is this what we can expect from you, too?"

My brother wanted to take his case before the judge, so naturally I was summoned to court and a number of false witnesses were called in to testify against me. Before I left home, I told Menalu to be strong and brave. "I do not know if I will be returning," I told her, "but I need you to be strong for the children. God has helped us this far. We must continue to trust Him now."

When I walked into the courtroom, I was not afraid.

Lawyers for the Interior Ministry looked very serious, confident, like a lion sure of the capture of its prey, but I was not afraid. Orthodox Ethiopians filled the seats, already condemning me with their presence and their glances, but I was not afraid. I was called before the judge.

"Are you Kokeb Gedamu?"

"Yes, I am Kokeb Gedamu?"

"Do you believe in *Yeshu*?"

"No, I do not believe in *Yeshu*."

"You don't believe in *Yeshu*?" he asked incredulously.

"No, I do not," I said.

"Then what is your faith?"

Yeshu was the cursed, derogatory name that the Israelis had given to *Yeshua*. "I believe in *Yeshua*," I said confidently.

"What is the difference?" he asked.

"Yeshua is the Savior. I do not know anything about the other," I said, speaking fluently in the Hebrew I had learned over the last five years.

"Then you believe in Jesus?" he asked, using the English pronunciation.

"Yes, I believe in Jesus."

"But Jewish people don't believe in Jesus."

"That is not my problem," I said. "I believe in the God of Abraham, the God of Isaac, and the God of Jacob." I had my Bible with me, so I brought it forth and turned to Jeremiah 31:31 and read it. Then I turned to Isaiah 53 and read it to the Israeli judge, the Interior Ministry lawyers, and the Orthodox

Ethiopian Jews who were present. "I believe that our God revealed Himself as Yeshua, our Saviour."

"You are accused of corrupting the youth," he said parrying my declaration. "It is against the law to give money to young people bribing them into changing their faith. Do you know that you could be sentenced to a prison term from five to fifteen years?"

"I am not a criminal," I told the judge. "I did not steal. I have not taken anyone's life, and I did not give anyone money, yet you call me a criminal."

"We have a video of you giving money to young people? You also brought missionaries from outside. Are you the leader of this underground organization?

"No, I do not have an underground ministry. We are legal; we have an *amutta*. We believe the same God that our forefathers believed, and I am not alone in my faith. If you want, I can bring you many American Jews who believe in Yeshua. They don't have any of these problems that I am having. But me—because I am poor and I am black, that is why they are accusing me." I had resolved before I walked through the door of the courtroom that I was willing to go to prison; if need be, I was willing to die for the Gospel.

Many men and women had stood where I was now standing. The Greatest Man of All had heard the same words that I heard, but He had been sentenced to death. Still he did not recant. He had brought me to this moment. I would not deny Him or my faith.

"I am willing to go to jail," I told him, "but I want you to know that this will be a story written all over the world. I will make sure that newspapers and television and radio stations hear about it and then let the readers and listeners judge the wrong I have done. Let them judge me a criminal."

"We will review your case," the judge said, "so you may go home for now."

In the meantime, Torch of Gideon had demoted me as their leader, claiming that I caused too much trouble for them. They changed the office locks, calling me an employee.

"I am a minister of God and will be whatever he wants me to be," I told them. "I helped to form this organization and you cannot make major changes without my input."

Hurt, wounded and realizing they would not relent, I said, "Do whatever you want. It does not matter." Although I felt great abandonment, I still continued to serve the congregation in my new capacity.

The Interior Ministry called in every Ethiopian Messianic believer who had attended the conference to their headquarters and showed them the videos to frighten them. They said to each one as they said to me, "You are a missionary. If you do not stop what you are doing, we will deport you from Israel and revoke your citizenship." The believers were frightened. They had come from some of the remotest villages in Ethiopia, and did not know their rights. Instead of standing together, we fought against each other.

"You have hurt our movement," the elders told me,

"and you have not listened to us. As discipline, you are suspended for six months." "Suspension" meant that I would receive a salary but I could not function as a minister.

While I was a leader in Torch of Gideon, in 1997 Dr. Robert and Tara Winer had come to Israel and met the leaders in the underground congregation. They were from Philadelphia, Pennsylvania. I could see their great love for *Yeshua,* so we connected right away. We invited these American Messianic Jews into our home and prepared Ethiopian food, complete with *injera,* vegetables, and a spicy beef. Although Tara could not adjust to the spiciness, Robert, who wanted to be called Bob had no problems enjoying it with Menalu, the children, and me.

Dr. Winer invited me to join him at the Messiah Conference sponsored by the Messianic Jewish Alliance Association in Grantham, PA in 1998, the following year. He said that I would meet a number of Messianic believers who had found a greater degree of freedom to practice their faith.

When the persecution in Israel started, I called Dr. Winer and shared with him the difficulty that I was experiencing. As a man of discernment, he pointed out to me that friction had arisen in my congregation because of the difference in vision. "Whenever there are two separate visions in one congregation, there will always be strife," he explained. "They wanted to stay underground. You wanted to go public. They wanted to move slowly. You wanted to move fast." He understood! When he gave that explanation, it reminded me of the Jerusalem congregation in the first century during the Apostle Paul's day. Their concentration was Jerusalem. It was the congregation in Antioch Syria that sent Paul out as a missionary into Asia Minor. Jerusalem and Antioch had different visions, but all leaning toward the same goal. I was able to understand my brothers and why they did what they did. I prayed that they could understand me and my motives, as well.

Dr. Winer invited my family and me to come to Canada. "Enroll at the World Impact Bible Institute," he said. "Stay for two years. You do not have to worry about funding. I will take care of everything." Canada would be a long awaited respite from the severe trials and testing of my faith. And as Apostle Paul had to do when his presence brought undue persecution upon a congregation, he moved on…so I would move on. I could get away from the persecution, get refreshed in the Spirit, and get the Biblical training that I needed. Little did I know that Canada would also be the launching pad for even greater blessings.

Chapter 19

Canada—Toronto & St Catherine, December 1999

I COULD NOT BELIEVE THAT I WAS BOARDING A PLANE TO TAKE ME away from the place I had spent most of my life and energy getting to. It was a bittersweet parting—some in Congregation Torch of Gideon wept; others knew that this might have been the time for the congregation to dispense with its inner strife and heal. I knew that it was a time for me to grow as well.

We arrived in Toronto in the winter, around Christmas time. Rabbi Jeffrey and Janet Forman, our new American Messianic Jewish friends, picked us up at the airport and took us to the apartment they had provided for us in St. Catherines. They were the founders and leaders of City of David Messianic Congregation in Toronto, Canada. Dr. Winer introduced them to us at the Messiah Conference 1998 in Grantham, PA, and after that we had many phone conversations. Rabbi Forman and Dr.

Winer together had encouraged my family and me to come to Canada and attend the same Bible college that Rabbi Forman had attended. They had solicited their congregation for furniture and everything else that we needed to be comfortable in our new home, and they welcomed us into their congregation. We were now ready to settle in.

Before I could mature through Biblical training, I received an education in Canadian weather. Menalu had asked me to buy milk for Tsiona. We did not have a car, so I decided to walk. I had seen a corner store as Rabbi Forman drove us to our new home. I looked outside. It was sunny, and I could feel the warmth of the sun's rays through the windowpane against my face, so I knew that I would have a pleasant walk. Once outside, I realized that the sun had deceived me because it was freezing. I had no jacket and no gloves, but I continued to walk. The more I walked, the more my fingers and toes tingled. I arrived at the store and hurried in, very grateful for the warmth. After paying for the milk, I headed out the store, dreading the return trip.

I picked up my pace, but the wind seemed to possess icy shards that pierced my skin. I honestly did not know if my toes were still in my shoes. The only way that I knew that I still had fingers was because I could see them. I could hardly let go of the plastic bag in my hand when I entered our apartment. I hurried to the sink, and instead of putting cold water on my hands (as someone told me much later I should have done), I turned the water up as hot as I could get it. Pain radiated through my whole body, so I tried to warm my hands naturally. Although I did not have serious frostbite, the experience was enough to prepare and my family and me for the cold.

The adjustment to Canada was difficult. The children could not speak English, so when they started school, they felt like outsiders. But we encouraged them to persevere and to see themselves the way God saw them. I had to encourage myself as well because I had started at the Bible institute and knew that I could not give up, especially because I was an example for them. I had learned to speak English, Arabic, and Hebrew. I was receiving Biblical education in English. There was much at stake, so I had to excel.

The weather was harsh with blizzards hurling knee-deep snow in our midst. This was the first we heard of the "flu season," but our children were able to stay healthy despite the weather and their sick classmates. We considered that another miracle! Menalu was not able to work or attend school because she had to take care of Tsiona who was not quite ready for kindergarten. In addition to the weather, we missed our family and did not find an Ethiopian community or congregation in Canada. We felt very alone. Seasons came and went in our lives, so I knew that this season of winter and loneliness had to pass as well.

Bob and Tara bought us a car so that we could travel easily about. I had driven in Israel, but the streets of the Promised Land were not to be compared to the highways of

Canada. Before I could get the gist of driving on them, I stopped on major highways to read a map and traveled at a snail's pace to cars honking me as they zoomed past.

When friends from Germany and Israel realized we were in Canada, they came to visit us. Some Canadian students that I met at the Bible institute came to our house to fellowship over meals. God provided for us so that we could be a blessing to as many who had been a blessing to us. A German benefactor Dr. Freisman supported us financially. Dr. Winer told us about Rabbi Frank and Margaret Lowinger of congregation Brit Hadoshah in Buffalo, NY. He was a member of the MJAA and invited me to his congregation to speak. Taking the trips into Buffalo was a welcomed deviation from our normal routine. We had an opportunity to meet other Messianic believers, I had a chance to share some of what I learned at the institute, and I got more experience driving on the highway.

Menalu wanted to attend Bible school with me, but we thought it best if she went to beauty school. We felt that she could be an encouragement to Ethiopian women when we returned to Israel. She could also hire women to work for her and train more women to start their own businesses. And her vocation would be additional funding for the support of our ministry.

In St. Catherine, Menalu enrolled in beauty school. Although I knew this would be beneficial, I was concerned about the difficulty. For two months, fellow students ridiculed her because of her accent. Although at times she was so discouraged she wanted to stop, she knew that she could not. We had paid a great deal for her tuition, and she knew that it would not be a good witness for the children. Because of her perseverance and determination, in three months she was first in her class. Then in a promotion, she was asked to assist other classmates.

In two years, I completed my studies at the Bible institute and Menalu at the beauty school, so I decided that we should return to Israel. Menalu was totally opposed to returning. "In two years," she said, "we cannot forget what happened to us in Israel. It is very hard to forget and it's even harder to forgive."

I understood how she felt, but Israel was our home. We had a congregation there. I, however, went back to Israel to visit and took a Canadian friend with me. The congregation was happy to see me and welcomed me with open arms. Some of them wept. "After you left," they said, "there has been no revival, nothing has happened! Please come back," they pleaded.

Caught up in the idealized pleasure of that moment, I told them that my family and I would return in two weeks. I knew that when I told Menalu about the reception and their desire for our return that she would want to return as well. When I arrived home, I told Menalu that we would return to Israel in two weeks. She said, "I have already said that it would be hard for me to go back. You have to make a choice.

Choose me and your family or Israel."

I was facing a new dilemma. She had never given me an ultimatum and had always respected my leading. I knew that I could not stay in Canada after my student visa had expired. If I did, I would have to continue my studies.

Seemingly, out of nowhere, Menalu said, "We have to go to America."

"How can we do that?" I asked, as if her wish were impossible. In my mind it was. "We do not have visas," I told her. We had tried two times to go to America, but my family was always rejected. I had a tourist visa. I could visit but I could not work there. For three days we fasted and prayed. At the end of the fast, I called Dr. Winer and asked his advice. "Your wife is right," he said. Listen to her. The first priority is your family. Don't confuse your children too much. Your family has lived in an Arab country. They have lived in Israel. They spoke Hebrew, now English."

"Dr. Winer," I said, "why should I listen to her when there is no way we can stay in Canada?"

"Let's see what we can do," he said.

After a while, I called Dr. Winer and asked him if he knew of any way we could come to America. He said he was checking around to see if he could find a sponsor for us.

"If we do," he said, "you could come here and start your own congregation and be a part of the Messianic movement here." He had a nonprofit ministry but not his own congregation to sponsor us.

When Rabbi Lowinger in Buffalo, NY heard about my family's plight, he and his congregation took the responsibility of sponsoring us spiritually, and Dr. Winer supported us financially. He also gathered all the paperwork and sent it to us to complete. We could not believe the stack of papers, almost two inches thick. It was intimidating enough for us to lose hope and say forget it; we were never getting into America. Had the last two years caused me to forget about the impossibilities God had brought us out of?! Dr. Winer then called us to tell us that we had an appointment in Toronto at the American Embassy.

We gathered the huge stack and nervously went to the Embassy. The officer called me in and told my family to remain in the waiting area. I sat before him and handed him the application. He read the first page, skimmed the others, issued us passports, and granted us three-year visas. "Pay the money," he said. After almost two years in Canada, we were going to start a new life in America, which would bring with it new challenges all its own.

Chapter 20

America—Philadelphia, Pennsylvania, 2001

In the 16th Chapter of Acts, Paul tried to sail into Bythynia, but the Holy Spirit did not allow him to. I often wonder what indication the Holy Spirit gave him—a still, small voice; a cautious spouse saying, "Choose me or Bythynia"; a wise friend saying, "Don't confuse your companions"; impossible situations; or a customs officer who quelled his fears. For me it was all the above, and as a result, my family and I began the next phase of our lives in America in September 2001.

We loaded our car and drove over 1,500 miles into Philadelphia. Dr. Winer rented a three-bedroom apartment for us in Narbreth, a suburb of Philadelphia and part of Lower Merrion school district. Pastor Seifu Kebde, my spiritual father, introduced me to a woman who was a believer and lived in

Philadelphia. She, my family, I and three others started an all-night prayer meeting in our home. This was the beginning of the congregation I established called Congregation Burning Bush of Greater Philadelphia. We contacted other Ethiopians who were flying in from neighboring cities in Pennsylvania and other states like Oklahoma to help. We passed out flyers, and I went around sharing my testimony wherever I could. In three years we had eighty-five members, ninety-eight percent of whom were believers in Jesus but not Jewish.

I went to Denver for two weeks to give a marriage seminar and left one of my ministers in charge. This man to whom I had given responsibility to lead the congregation started slandering me. He said that I was not really Ethiopian. I was Jewish and should be a part of the Messianic movement. Therefore what I was preaching was not a good religion to follow. "You don't have to follow him," he told them. Then the congregation became divided. This is the man whom I interceded for and counseled, and the Lord used me to save his marriage and his life. In America, I was being persecuted because I was Jewish. In Israel it was because I was a Christian. It was all very different for me but a huge awakening about the ways of the world.

However, as always, in the midst of persecution, the Lord did miraculous things in America. He gave me favor at Beth Yeshua Congregation in Philadelphia led by Rabbi David and Debra Chernoff. My children grew up in the *kehillat,* and Beth Yeshua became part of our family. They opened their door and lives to us. They allowed me to preach and minister to my brothers and sisters in that congregation. While there, I took *yeshiva* courses for two years and was ordained as a Messianic Rabbi at International Alliance of Messianic Congregations and Synagogues (IAMCS). Under MJAA, I was appointed as Chairman of Operation Tikvah, the department overseeing Ethiopian Jewry. I was put in charge of African Ministries under IAMCS as the regional director, a rabbinic office.

In 2004 I established House of Israel International Ministry (HIIM), a nonprofit ministry that serves the Beta Yisrael around the world, especially those left in Ethiopia. The Lord brought me to America so that I could tell our story and reach out across the continent to help my brothers. Until then, HIIM helps to make life bearable for the Beta Yisrael by digging wells in their villages.

HIIM provides humanitarian aid, medical and spiritual support to indigenous *Beta Yisrael*, saving many young and old from malaria and other diseases. Because more than 130,000 *Beta Yisrael* are impeded from economic success in Israel because of cultural and linguistic barriers, HIIM seeks to establish technical schools so that the *Beta Yisrael* can be trained to compete with other Israelis for jobs and positions. Since the older generation does not fully understand the value of education, they do not encourage the younger generation who are eventually satisfied with minimum-waged jobs. Even though they are afforded government scholarships to colleges, they rarely graduate because they are ill prepared. With preparatory training, the young *Beta Yisrael* can become productive citizens and strengthen the Israeli economy.

HIIM seeks to bridge the ever-widening gap between the older generation of *Beta Yisrael* who still hold on to rural moral codes and the younger generation entrenched in a modern society.

I published two books in Amharic on marriage entitled Marriage Life and After the Honeymoon in hopes that these books would minister to marriages caught in a culture shock. Many marriages were healed and my compatriots were blessed by the books. Currently they are being translated into English and are due out in print at the time of the printing of this book.

My wife won a three-story house, in which we currently live, when she entered a drawing that a builder was using as a promotional for a new housing development. We were able to enroll our children in private school because the Lord raised up people who provided money for their tuition and school supplies. Porsha Scholl was such a person. As soon as we walked into Beth Yeshua, she saw our children, fell in love with them, and committed to be their *sabeta*, which means grandmother in Hebrew. To this day they call her *Sabeta* Porsha. Her involvement in their lives meant a lot to us and the children, especially since their maternal grandmother was living in Ethiopia.

After several years in private school, our children felt they were ready to attend public school, and the Lord provided Godly friends and favor. Eight years later after arrival in

America, my wife and children have work permits and have applied for green cards. Ruhama completed high school as an honor roll student, and is in college. Although unable to receive federal aid or scholarships, the Lord has been faithful in providing her every educational need. Ruhama's dream is to work with me in the ministry and return to Israel to live. She still practices her Hebrew, hoping that one day her dream will be realized.

After fifteen years, we miraculously found Mr. Southersby, the one who helped us out of Sudan! He was the political attache who was our Moses! He came to Ruhama's graduation and ate with us in our home.

✡✡✡✡✡✡✡✡✡✡✡✡✡✡✡✡✡✡✡✡✡✡✡

Four countries, three continents and over a million miles from a little hut in Mo'ta I have come, but I have never been alone. The events that brought me here were not coincidence or "luck" as some would label them. It was the hand of the Almighty who spoke over me the night I was born; He called me "light—kokeb." His Spirit gathered people, orchestrated events, and touched hearts in various places so that the "light" could be enhanced.

He gathered the oil, the wick, the globe, the fire for "kokeb"...from the little Orthodox village church in Mo'ta, the thriving city of Gondar, the quiet town of Debre Markos, the bustling city of Addis Ababa, the craggy sides of the Blue Nile

Gorge, the sugar canes of Wonja Showa, the *ferenge-och* of Bahar Dar, the border village of Sudan, Dr. Henok from Germany, Esther from Switzerland, the generous congregation of Finland, underground congregations in Israel, and the frigid walls of Canada...and I am eternally grateful for His faithfulness and incredible mercies.

As the Israelites were commanded to leave twelve stones in the Jordan as the Lord parted it for them to cross, so have we left such stones in the places we have been, commemorating the miracles of our lives.

I leave my sisters Abren and Assegedech in Mo'ta, Ethiopia. The former is a housewife with three children, the latter a widow with one child and an administrator in Mo'ta High School.

In Gondar, I leave Rekebenaha, a very successful matriarch of her own private school.

In Sudan, the memory of the birth of our Ruhama, God's unending mercies to us from the border town of Tiha to the capital city of Khartoum.

In Egypt, the memory of the birth of Ebenezer, for the Lord brought us from being wandering refugees to servants in the home of an American diplomat.

In Israel, the memory of the birth of Tsiona, the fulfillment of a dream imagined by all *Beta Yisrael*, and my fated connection with Messianic Jews.

In Canada, the milestone of a religious education for

me, and my brother Libanos who is now a Canadian citizen.

In America…abounding favor…and…

our ***journey beyond imagination*** still continues…

RESOURCES

If you would like to obtain more information about the subjects below, visit the websites that follow:

Beta Yisrael
[1]http://www.jewishvirtuallibrary.org/jsource/Judaism/ejhist.html
www.iaej.co.il/pages/history_in_the_beginning.htm

Felash Mura
http://www.jewishvirtuallibrary.org/jsource/Judaism/falashmura.html

Coptic Orthodox Church
www.copticchurch.net

Ethiopian Orthodox Church
www.ethiopianorthodox.org

Messianic Jewish Alliance Association (MJAA)
www.mjaa.org

House of Israel International Ministry (HIIM)
www.hoisrael.org

[2](www.nationalanthems.info)

Map from Ezilon.com used by permission.

CONTACT INFORMATION

If you would like to contact Rabbi Kokeb Gedamu, invite him to speak at your congregation, donate to his ministry, or discover more about House of Israel Ministries (HIIM), please visit, write or call:

House of Israel International Ministry, Inc.

P. O. Box 461262

Aurora, CO 80046

Telephone: +1 720 987 9951

E-mail:

info@hoisrael.org

Website:

www.hoisrael.org

Kokeb Gedamu:

Cell Phone: 720-987-9951

E-mail: kogedamu@gmail.com

ABOUT THE AUTHOR

Rev. Juanita Weiss received a B.A. from Norfolk State University in English Education, an M.A. from Regent University in Communications, and a degree in Biblical Studies from Bible Teachers Institute.

She is a retired educator from the Virginia Beach City Public Schools. Having served as the president of Tidewater Bible College, she is a consummate Bible teacher, conference speaker, and workshop leader.

As an author, she published the booklet *Mary and Martha: Jesus' Worship and Praise Team*. She is set to print an inspirational book entitled *God* ***Still*** *Uses Vessels*, and various manuals, like *Women in Ministry*, and a series of devotionals.

As a playwright, she wrote and produced a number of highly acclaimed plays, one of them published, *Satan's Assignment: Canceled*. She produced a quarterly magazine, *Touching His Heart*, and hosted a radio broadcast–"The Master Calls." She and her husband David founded Weiss Ministries, Inc., which serves as a bridge between diverse cultures, connecting them through education, publications, performing arts, and missions—local and foreign.

For ten years she provided servant leadership as Pastoral Liaison and Director of Ministries to fifteen ministries at Tidewater Bibleway Temple in Portsmouth, VA.

An ordained minister with Evangelical Christian Alliance, she currently serves under Rabbi Joseph Rosenfarb with her husband Elder David Weiss in leadership capacity at Beth Messiah Synagogue in Norfolk, VA.

To contact her or to request more information on her ministry, visit her website at www.weissministries.com or friend request her on Facebook.